"Identity is the most significant issue facing young people today because it's foundational to every aspect of their lives and directly relates to the most prominent issues in our culture. In *Iconic*, my friend Mike McGarry provides a helpful resource that connects the theological dots with theological, spiritual, and practical implications of grounding our understanding of identity in the image of God."

> **R. Scott Pace,** Provost, Dean of Graduate Studies, Jim Shaddix Chair of Expository Preaching, Professor of Preaching and Pastoral Ministry, SEBTS

"Mike McGarry is respected nationally because of his theological precision and for keeping student ministry grounded in Scripture. Thus, he is just the right one to address the timely topic of identity—first as human beings and then as individuals. We will all celebrate when Mike's young readers begin to declare: 'We are living icons, pointing to the greater reality of who God is and what he's like.'"

> **Richard Ross,** Senior Professor of Student Ministry, Southwestern Seminary, Fort Worth, TX

"Christians often say that humans are made in the image of God, but what does that actually mean? McGarry explores how the foundational truth of image-bearing establishes our identity, guides our thinking, and forms our relationships with God, self, and others. Profound, pastoral, and practical, *Iconic* will bless both teenagers and the adults who read it with them."

> **Anna Meade Harris,** Senior Director of Content, Rooted Ministry; author of *God's Grace for Every Family*

"Mike McGarry leads readers through challenging issues facing youth and young adults today, providing a much-needed theological grounding to the journey. Neither simplistic nor unnecessarily complicated, *Iconic* reminds readers of the dignity and goodness of human life created and restored in the image of God."

Graham Stanton, Director, Ridley Centre for
Children's and Youth Ministry, Melbourne, Australia

"With biblical clarity and pastoral sensitivity, *Iconic* explains what it means to be made in God's image. It also addresses tensions, questions, and objections that accompany issues like sexuality and gender with wisdom and care. Moreover, every chapter is grounded in the gospel of grace. I wouldn't hesitate to hand this book to any teenager or young adult."

Jonathan K. Dodson, Founder, GCdiscipleship.com;
author of *Gospel-Centered Discipleship*

"Mike McGarry not only helps readers understand and delight in the truth of their being made in God's image but also equips them to grow as thoughtful, faithful readers of Scripture. Along the way, he masterfully models how to connect the dots theologically, making this a deeply formative, engaging, and timely read."

Danielle (Dani) Treweek, Author of *Single Ever After*; Sydney Anglican Diocesan Research Officer

"In *Iconic*, Mike McGarry sets young people on the course of discovering who they truly are, giving them the sure foundation on which to see, understand, and navigate all of life to the glory of their identity-giving Maker! This book is a roadmap for human flourishing in a culture of mass identity confusion."

Walt Mueller, President, Center for Parent/Youth Understanding

"Being made in the image of God is a beautiful truth that all believers should understand and live out on a daily basis to impact the world around them for the glory of God. This book can help you do that. Get this for yourself and get copies to hand out as a blessing to others."

Shane Pruitt, National Next Gen Director, North American Mission Board (NAMB); author of *Calling Out the Called*

ICONIC
Being God's Image in Your World

Mike McGarry

New
Growth
Press

newgrowthpress.com

New Growth Press, Greensboro, NC 27401
newgrowthpress.com
Copyright © 2025 by Mike McGarry

Unless otherwise indicated, Scripture quotations are taken from Holy Bible, New International Version®, NIV® Copyright © 1973, 1978, 1984, 2011 by Biblica, Inc.® Used by permission. All rights reserved worldwide.

Scripture verses marked ESV are taken from The Holy Bible, English Standard Version. ESV® Text Edition: 2016. Copyright © 2001 by Crossway Bibles, a publishing ministry of Good News Publishers.

Cover Design: Derek Thornton
Interior Typesetting/Ebook: Lisa Parnell
Series Editor: Samuel L. Bierig

ISBN: 978-1-64507-513-4 (paperback)
ISBN: 978-1-64507-514-1 (ebook)

Library of Congress Cataloging-in-Publication Data on file

Printed in the United States of America

29 28 27 26 25   1 2 3 4 5

Dedication

To my mother, Nancy, whose life
bears God's image so beautifully

Contents

Introduction

What Does It Mean to Be Iconic?

What do you want your life to represent? This is an important question to ask on multiple levels. We all want to leave a legacy—to contribute something meaningful and enduring with our lives—and this existential desire prompts us toward clarity about what we hope that legacy will become. A more basic level of this question has to do with the way we want others to think about us.

It seems like everyone today is talking about "identity" and discovering *Who am I?* Discovering your identity helps you know what you want your life to represent. It gives you direction for decision-making and helps you find a like-minded community of people who share your values and purpose. But most of these conversations about identity overlook the foundation of who we are: our humanity. How in the world can we answer *Who am I?* if we never answer *What am I?* Understanding our identity as human beings is foundational for understanding our identity as individuals. That's why I've written this book: I want to help you discover what it means that you are created in the image of God so you can live an iconic life that represents him faithfully in your world.

It's easy to curate your social media profile to make yourself look however you want, even if it's not an honest representation of who you really are. A selfie here, a collaboration there, and carefully selecting your likes can portray you to be whomever you want to be. You get to craft your own image. But that only changes people's perception of you, not your actual identity. This is why so many of your peers look like they're living their best lives even though they're struggling with insecurity or loneliness or fear. They are so focused on how they appear that they don't really know who they are.

The Bible tells us that God created people in his image. The Greek word that's used for *image* in the New Testament is the word *eikon*, which is where we get the English word *icon*. People are living "icons" of God in this world. That leads us to a helpful and understandable way to think about what it means to be created in the image of God: We are iconic of God. We are living icons, pointing to the greater reality of who God is and what he's like. This book will lead you through Scripture to explore and apply what that means for you and me.

In short, the question this book seeks to address is this: What does it mean to live as icons of Christ in this world?

What Is the Image of God Anyway?

The Bible teaches that God created people "in the image of God." Genesis 1:26–27 says, "Then God said, 'Let us make mankind in our image, in our likeness.' . . . So God created mankind in his own image, in the image of God he created them; male and female he created them."

One of the most foundational ways we bear God's image is through the attributes we share with him. We are like God in many ways. God is the Creator, and so we create. God exists in eternal community within himself, and we crave community with one another. Chapter 8 will explore the "communicable attributes" in further detail. They are traits that every person shares, to some degree, with God: love, knowledge, wisdom, goodness, etc. In this way, we bear God's image within our humanity, even though many take these traits for granted as evolutionary survival skills. In this regard, bearing God's image means that every person is actually like God because he created us with some of his own attributes embedded into our human nature. This God-given dignity has led some to believe people are divine themselves, with no need for God at all. As ironic as that is, even this false view of humanity displays that the innate glory and honor God has given to his image-bearers is obvious to all, even those who may deny his existence. In this sense, we don't simply bear God's image—we are his image in this world.[1] This is an irremovable characteristic of what it means to be human.

The book of Genesis was originally written in Hebrew. Two Hebrew words in Genesis 1:26–27 point to two sides of the same truth about how and why God created humanity: *tzelem*, meaning "image" and *demuth*, meaning "likeness." A *tzelem* was a physical representation that a king would set up to remind people about his power and authority (see Daniel 3:1). Being made in

God's image and likeness means men and women were created as God's representatives to uniquely carry out his ongoing work in creation. Our very existence is a living reminder of God's reign and glory and provision.

Every person bears the image of God. The "image of God" is both what we are and what we do. It's embedded within what it means to be a human being. God created us to be and to bear his image in a way that lifts others' eyes to behold his character and goodness in us. Sin has affected our ability to do this, but it hasn't removed the God-given dignity he wove into our humanity. The worst sinner remains God's *tzelem* in this world, in the sense that *what they are* is a living reminder of his divine nature and goodness in this world. Everyone bears God's image, but sin has corrupted the way we bear it, so we seek our own glory and build our own kingdoms. Through the gospel, God's image-bearers are forgiven of their sin and conformed into the image of God through faith in the person and work of Jesus Christ. Christians bear God's glory according to God's good design in order that all creation would see our good works and give glory to our Father in heaven (Matthew 5:16).

WHY THE IMAGE OF GOD MATTERS FOR YOU

Nearly every controversial issue in our culture today finds its resolution in the image of God. If the Bible's message is true and God created humans in his image, then it radically transforms the way Christians approach issues like racism, gender and sexuality, abortion, mental health, injustice, disability, and euthanasia, among others. This biblical foundation shifts the conversation away from a matter of opinion and toward what human flourishing (for individuals and cultures to be healthy and full of joy) looks like according to our Creator's good design. For example, racism is sinful and wrong because of the way it fundamentally undermines what it means to be a human being, not merely because of the harm it causes to individuals. The same principle applies to gender identity and abortion and a host of other issues. This isn't an attempt to provide a simplistic answer to complicated issues. But without understanding the biblical message about men and women as image-bearers, we're left without a firm foundation for these important issues.

Understanding the image of God is the missing link in the many conversations about identity. It's like we're trying to figure out our individual stories without realizing that we're characters in a bigger story that's being told. God's story for humanity begins in creation, has important chapters throughout that helps us understand what's gone wrong, and it gives us hope to endure because the story ends in glory. God created people to enjoy perfect intimacy with him and with one another as his image-bearers in this world.

Sin has twisted us so we're divided—against God and one another—and tempts us to take the glory of God's image and claim it as our own, trying to exert our power to establish our own kingdoms. But instead of giving up on us or abandoning us, God promised a Savior who came to restore the intimacy between God and people so that we would bear God's image well and be restored into relationship with each other too. One day, sin and the corruption it has introduced into the world will be wiped away, and we will live for all eternity in God's presence with perfect intimacy as his image-bearers. This is the bigger story that your identity fits into. Without it, you're left on your own to define your own reality and to choose your own adventure. Although this might sound like freedom, this mindset confines you to a life that's limited by your own wisdom, whereas embracing your God-given calling leads you into a life that is filled with God's steadfast love.

It's common to hear people talk about how iconic superstars like LeBron James or Taylor Swift represent the best in their respective fields. We, as God's image-bearers, are living icons of God in this world. People are God's living *tzelem* in his kingdom. We are living displays of God's glory and reign in his creation. This is why God commanded Israel, "You shall not make for yourself an image in the form of anything in heaven above or on the earth beneath or in the waters below. You shall not bow down to them or worship them" (Exodus 20:4–5).[2] Israel didn't need to create an image for God to remind them of his glory and presence because God had already placed his image among them!

It's so common to talk about identity in terms of *Who am I?*, but I want to encourage you to consider the question of identity through the question *What am I?* Until we ask that question, we'll continue to struggle to understand our identity. So many of the challenges we face today, as individuals and as a broader culture, flow from the reality that we've forgotten what it means to be a human being. The image of God doesn't merely inform how we are to act and treat others; it's an aspect of what we are as humans. As men and women who were created in God's image, you and I have God-given dignity and value that has nothing to do with what we do. Our dignity and value isn't determined by our GPA or resume; it's built into us as icons of the living God who is King over creation. The way God created us as his image-bearers has a direct impact on our relationships.

QUESTIONS FOR REFLECTION

1. Have you ever thought about what it means for humans to be created in God's image? What does that phrase mean to you?

2. What do we lose when we forget that we are created in God's image? Why is this biblical message so important?

3. What does the author mean by "living an iconic life"? How does this flow from being created in God's image?

Chapter 1
Iconic Relationships

Y ou were created for relationships. The first thing God declared "not good" was Adam's loneliness in Genesis 2:18. Loneliness cuts so deep because it gets to the heart of what it means to bear God's image.

Christians believe in the Trinity. God is three-in-one. God the Father, God the Son, and God the Holy Spirit are wholly united (they cannot be separated), equal (they are equally God), and eternal (one did not create the others). This means God exists eternally in relationship within himself and is an inherently relational being. God has never been alone or lonely, and he didn't create humanity because he needed something from us. One of the central aspects of what it means to be created in God's image is the reality that we were created for relationships, because God is an eternally relational God.

It could be tempting to think the about the image of God as an abstract idea, but nothing could be further from the truth. In this section, I want to set the table for you to begin seeing the ways the image of God shapes your daily relationships. Many of these ideas and themes will be picked up again and expanded upon in future chapters of the book. Embracing your identity as God's image-bearers will lead you to honor the Lord through four iconic relationships: with God, other people, creation, and yourself.

YOUR RELATIONSHIP WITH GOD

You were created to experience deep and intimate fellowship with God. You were created to bear God's image perfectly.

At first, Adam and Eve enjoyed perfect fellowship with God. They lived in the garden of Eden together and literally walked and talked with God. There was no need for a mediator or confession of sin. They didn't need to ask God for peace from their suffering or for healing from sickness. What we see in Genesis 1 and 2 is the perfect intimacy we were created to enjoy with God. What they were and how they lived was a perfect embodiment of their identity as God's image. They were perfectly iconic.

But temptation introduced suspicion in Adam and Eve toward God, leading them to question whether or not they wanted to be iconic or if they wanted to establish their own authority. That's what sin is, really. It's an expression of our suspicion against God, believing that he's holding us back by telling us we're merely image-bearers. Instead of being iconic, we want to be the authority. Sinful people aren't content to bear God's glory and to give God glory; we want to claim that glory for ourselves and to receive glory from others. That was at the root of the serpent's temptation of Adam and Eve, and it's still at the root of our temptations today.

Sin has led us to reject our identity as image-bearers. Instead of worshipping God because he is our Creator and worthy of our worship, we try setting the terms for our relationship with him. We have rightfully earned God's wrath, not because God is hot-headed and angry, but because we have rejected his laws and commandments and chosen to live according to our own desires. Our sinful nature has so twisted the image of God within us that instead of reflecting his glory and goodness in the world, we try to claim his glory and display our own goodness. This is why sin is so evil and carries such a heavy curse, because sin is a complete reversal of what it means for us to bear God's image.

The conflict and tension between God and humans continues today. Think about the people you know who reject God because they disagree with the way he's ordered creation. Many people today find it impossible to worship a God who claims there is only one path to salvation, who would judge sinners and tell them to deny themselves in order to honor him with their obedience. This is more than a disagreement with God; it's a rejection of what he says about us as his image-bearers.

An iconic relationship with God, however, is built on faith and worship: believing that he created us for perfect intimacy with himself, and that we find wholeness and fulfillment by remembering who God is (the holy Creator) and who we are (his image-bearers in this world). One of the most obvious signs of an iconic relationship with God is the way we treat other people.

Your Relationship with People

Sometimes nonreligious people dismiss the value of religion by saying things like, "All religions are basically the same because they all tell you to love people." But this is an incredibly simplistic way to summarize all religions. The basis for "love people" in various religions is remarkably different. For Christians, the reason we love others has nothing to do with seeking good karma or earning a seat at heaven's table. The Bible begins with our identity as men and women who are created in the image of God. Therefore we have an obligation to treat one another with dignity and honor.

There was no mistrust or suspicion between people until sin entered creation. The blame game began once Adam and Eve experienced the guilt of sin. Adam's strategy was to accuse both God and Eve for his sin by blaming "the woman you put here with me" (Genesis 3:12). Eve, on the other hand, blames the serpent for deceiving her. In a sense, both of them tell the truth. But neither of them takes responsibility for their sin. Instead of confession and repentance, there's a trail of finger-pointing, and the blaming hasn't stopped since that day.

Instead of living in holy fellowship with one another, we experience divisions and suspicion. One example of this is how the biblical message about the image of God leads Christians to resist the sin of racism and instead seek fellowship and unity across ethnic groups. Because all people are created in the image of God, we are called to honor that dignity. When we treat others with contempt, suspicion, or apathy because of their ethnicity, we are dishonoring their God-given dignity as fellow icons of God's glory. The Christian foundation for combating racism is built upon God's good design. Understanding the doctrine of the image of God calls us to live with iconic relationships that are built on a God-ordained foundation.

We were created to reflect the glory and goodness of God to one another. Instead, we sin against each other and even lead one another into temptation! When we do good and act selflessly, we often want recognition for it, as if doing what we were created to do should earn us an award. If we're honest, there are times when we serve others with sinful motives: It looks like we're doing a really good thing (like feeding the hungry) because we want others to think, *Wow, Mike is so kind!* We value those who can do something for us, while overlooking those who can't give us anything in return. This leads us to fake kindness and ulterior motives. How can we experience true fellowship with one another when selflessness and kindness is met with suspicion, wondering what the person *really* wants.

This isn't what iconic relationships should look like. The Bible calls us to love and honor and serve one another. When we sin against each other, we're supposed to confess our sin, repent, and forgive others who sin against us. Iconic relationships in a sinful and broken world are difficult and messy. But it is possible! This is what the church, as the family of God, is meant to be: a community of sinners who worship God together and lead one another to live in a way that brings him honor in the world. Living as faithful icons of Christ transforms not only our relationship with God and others, but our whole way of living in this world.

Your Relationship with Creation

Within God's blessing over his newly created image-bearers, God tells them to "rule over" the creatures, "fill the earth," and "subdue it" (Genesis 1:26, 28). This isn't permission to abuse the world or to use up all its resources. It is a God-given calling to rule it as his representatives. Caring for God's creation is something that is ingrained within humanity, like taming wild animals and building irrigation systems for better farming. Additionally, because God is the Creator it only makes sense that his image-bearers would create too. Using God's creation to make our own creations (like making tires from rubber trees and harnessing electricity to make light bulbs) is a beautiful fulfillment of Genesis 1:26–28. This is all part of what it means to subdue and rule over God's creation as his icons.

Unfortunately, there are times when I've taught about the Christian's relationship with creation, and faithful Christians assume I'm making a political statement. It's important for Christians to think biblically about the environment before they think about it politically. Sometimes people can think that conservatives only want to plunder the environment and liberals want to save the turtles. Nothing is further than the truth! Politics can be complicated, and it's not the point of this book at all. But caring for God's creation must be a real value for Christians because God has entrusted this creation to us, and we should not neglect what God has told us to do. This world matters. God created it. God will glorify it. We should treat it well. We'll explore this more in chapter 9.

Our relationship with creation goes beyond environmentalism. God created a world of beauty and order. God told Adam and Eve to care for and subdue the earth. That involves a calling to study and nurture the earth and to bring about fruitfulness. This is what farmers do when they plow their fields, add fertilizer, and irrigate the land so it produces crops. It's what scientists do when they forge new alloys, create medicines, or discover a new species. And it's what engineers and city planners do when they build cities for families and society to flourish. These are all expressions of humanity's relationship with creation. It is good for us to discover as much as we can about God's creation, to understand it, and to responsibly develop it in new and creative ways that bring God glory.

Whether you're teaching your dog a new trick, painting a picture, or applying for a nursing residency, Christians who recognize their identity as God's icons in this world will discover newfound joy in creation. Remember, God did not create because he needed anything. This means that sometimes God's artistically minded image-bearers will simply create for the joy of creation. Artists often resonate with God's creative nature in ways that enable them to create music and images that show us truths we've become blind toward. This joy can be found through a walk in the woods, painting a sunrise, looking at the stars on your telescope, or enjoying a morning fishing on the lake with a friend. These are all aspects of an iconic relationship with God's created order that bring him glory.

I hope it's clear by now that embracing your identity as God's icon in this world reaches into your whole life.

This leaves one final relationship that many Christians easily overlook: their relationship with themselves.

YOUR RELATIONSHIP WITH YOURSELF

God created you, and you matter to him. But God is God. He's not your therapist or life coach. He's not someone on the sidelines who steps in to patch you together when you get banged up. He is your Creator and his knowledge of you is personal and complete. The Bible teaches that "you [God] created my inmost being; you knit me together in my mother's womb" (Psalm 139:13). Jesus himself said that God pays such careful attention to each person that "the very hairs of your head are all numbered" (Luke 12:7). Knowing ourselves becomes much clearer when we know God, our Creator.

Some of us have a hard time with self-care. Others seem to focus so much on self-care that there's hardly any time or energy left for others. Both of those extremes are wrong. As an image-bearer, you are clothed in dignity. And that dignity ought to be treated with respect and faithfulness. That extends to the way you treat yourself and talk to yourself. Take some time to honestly ask yourself whether or not you tend to spend so much time caring for others because you're trying to avoid dealing with your own baggage, or if you are so focused on your own need for well-being that you've become self-obsessed. This can happen subtly and accidentally.

Some false teachers have twisted God's providing care to mean that strong faith will lead to strong health while weak faith leads to weak health, leading to the belief that if you have bad health then it's the result of your lack of faith. This is the message of the "prosperity gospel," and it isn't true at all. God doesn't work like a banker, who pays us with worldly health or financial wealth based upon our godliness and faith. Instead, Scripture shows us that the children of God often suffer in order that our faith would be put on display for others to see that God, and not our wealth or health, is our treasure.

Remembering your identity as God's image-bearer anchors who you are in what you are: a living embodiment of God's glory and goodness in this world. Our identity as God's icons is why the apostle Paul says our body is the temple of the Holy Spirit (1 Corinthians 6:19). This means your health matters to God. God created you so that his glory and goodness would be displayed through you.

That means he also created your body, and he designed it to work optimally a certain way. This is why we feel more stressed and depressed when we sit on the couch all day playing video games in a dark room while eating junk food, while an active lifestyle with a reasonable diet leads to lower stress levels. Obviously, this is a generalization and I'm not implying diet and exercise is the answer to every mental health problem, but it could be part of the solution because God created us as whole people. Your physical, mental, and sexual health are all connected. God created you that way. Exercise and a healthy lifestyle are one way to honor God by caring for the body he has given you.

What about sickness, disability, and mental health struggles? The next chapter addresses this question, but it's important to recognize these are realities in our broken and sinful world. Personal sin isn't always at the root of these challenges, but the very existence of sin has corrupted creation and is the reason why things aren't the way they were in Eden. All creation bears the scar of sin. That extends into creation in general (e.g., hurricanes, droughts, and earthquakes) and to people (e.g., cancer, autism, bipolar disorder). None of us have perfect health anymore, but we walk by faith, trusting that our heavenly Father is caring for us in this broken world and will restore us into whole and holy health in glory.

Your relationship with yourself is strengthened by remembering what you are as a human being, created in God's image. You can endure hardships and suffering in this life because you have great confidence in who God is, who you are, and what's to come for you.

Gospel Clarity: Becoming Truly Iconic

As you read this book and consider what the Bible teaches about the nature and destiny of humanity, it's important to apply that knowledge personally. It's also important to remember that you won't become iconic by trying really hard. You'll become iconic by keeping your eyes on Jesus and walking in him. All four of these relationships described above are completely transformed by Jesus Christ.

God created people in his image, and he didn't walk away or abandon us after we sinned. Incredibly, even in the midst of God's judgment on Adam and Eve's sin, he promised a future Savior who would crush the head of the tempter (Genesis 3:15). And when the time was right, he didn't merely send another prophet or good teacher; he sent Jesus Christ, the very image of God (Colossians 1:15). Through Christ's death and resurrection, our sin has been conquered and paid for. Through his ascension and the gift of the Holy Spirit, we have been transformed into the image of Christ. And when he returns, he will finish the work of salvation and we will live in perfect fellowship with God and one another in the new heavens and new earth. Sinners have been saved through Jesus Christ.

Gospel clarity sets us free. Our relationship with God has been restored by his own initiative through Jesus Christ, so we can embrace our identity as sons and daughters of God. The focus of our relationships with others gradually shifts from seeking ways to use people to instead seeking ways to love and serve them as an expression of our worship to God. Our relationship with creation is full of joy and wonder, even as we await its restoration. And our relationship with ourselves brings wisdom and patience as we desire to honor the Lord with our whole selves. Our whole life has stopped being about us and our kingdom-building. Now, it's about living in a way that embodies the glory and goodness of God in our world so others will find their wholeness in Christ.

Now that we've seen how the image of God transforms our relationships, it's necessary to ask how this message applies to our gender and sexuality.

Questions for Reflection

1. Which of those four relationships do you tend to overlook most frequently? Why?
2. Christians don't often talk about our relationship with nature as an expression of our relationship with

God. What about this idea stands out as something you want to embrace or discuss with someone else?

3. Think about your relationships with family and friends. What are some challenges you face in building iconic relationships?

Chapter 2
Iconic Identity

Living as God's icon in this world means that your whole life matters. That includes your gender and sexuality. This is obviously a difficult topic to talk about, and it's filled with potential land mines. So let's make a deal: I'll do my best to write honestly and clearly, without making unfair assumptions or harsh judgments, and you'll do your best to take what I say at face value without making unfair assumptions or harsh judgments about what you think I might *really* mean or about what could have been worded better.

Forgetting *what* we are leads to confusion about *who* we are. Nowhere is this truer than in today's discussions of gender identity and sexual expression. And this applies to everyone, not only the LGBTQ+ community. Younger generations are increasingly identifying as nonbinary or as something other than their birth gender. Young people also navigate an online world that's filled with porn. Older generations continue to experience the fallout of our culture's divorce epidemic. We all need to understand the biblical definitions of humanity and marriage if we are going to understand our own sexual desires and how to live as men and women who honor God.

As a longtime youth pastor in Massachusetts (the first state in the United States to legalize gay marriage) and a dad of two teenagers, I know how costly it is for teenagers and young adults to hold onto biblical convictions about gender and sexuality. Honestly, it's more costly for you to remain faithful in these conversations than it is for your parents' and grandparents' generations. Despite this, I want to assure you that God sees your faithfulness and he will be with you. Whatever the cost is for you personally, your reward in Christ is far greater.

Let's start by laying my cards on the table. First, I believe the Bible teaches God created two genders, male and female, and these are not merely social constructs. Yes, each culture has different norms for masculinity and femininity that we shouldn't equate with what it means to be a man or woman. And yes, some people are born intersex and others experience same-sex attraction or gender dysphoria from a young age. But those realities are painful reminders that this life bears the curse of sin until Jesus returns and makes all things new.

Second, I believe that biblical marriage is a covenant between one man and one woman and that sexual intimacy should be expressed only between a husband and wife. All other sexual activity is sinful: lust, pornography, sex among people who are not married to each other, etc. These views on gender and sexuality are rooted in

Scripture and represented throughout Christian history as the norm for what Christians believe about these issues.

WHAT THE BIBLE SAYS ABOUT MEN AND WOMEN

God created Adam first and then Eve. It should be obvious, but let's be very clear: Men and women bear God's image equally. Men are not more iconic than women, or vice versa. In the same way that men and women are biologically and genetically distinct but compatible, God created them to bear his image together while also creating them to bear his image differently. This doesn't only happen in marriage but also through friendship and community. Men and women need one another to build a culture that flourishes.

There isn't a singular biblical description of masculinity and femininity. People's expectations for what it looks like to "be a man" and "be a woman" are often driven by cultural expectations. For example, your great-grandmother's daily life and women's expectations today are remarkably different. Even today, a woman's life in America is going to be noticeably different from women's lives in, say, Uganda and China. This isn't because one country is better than the others, but because culture is different. There's a lot of room for what godly men and women can do with their time and vocations.

For example, Jacob and Esau were brothers: Esau was a hunter with rough hands and hairy arms, while Jacob would best be described as a "mama's boy" with soft skin. Yet God chose Jacob over his brother (Romans 9:13). David was "a man after his [God's] own heart" (1 Samuel 13:14) and was a warrior king who killed the giant Goliath; he also played the harp and wrote poetry (many of the psalms). Miriam is referred to as a prophet and led Israel in worship (Exodus 15:20–21) after the Lord dried up the Red Sea for their safe passage. Deborah was called to be a judge and to lead Israel in war against the Canaanites (Judges 4–5). Although people sometimes glorify the "Proverbs 31 woman" as a stay-at-home mom, this idealized individual worked hard and sold the family goods in the town's marketplace (vv. 13–18), which sounds a lot like a working mom to me!

The Bible isn't telling men to lead in ways that are harsh and demanding, and it isn't telling women they need to be quiet and passive. Both men and women need to follow God and bear his image faithfully. The rest of this section focuses on what the Bible says about husbands and wives—not because that's the pinnacle of manhood or womanhood, but because that's where we see the differences between men and women most clearly explained in Scripture.

The Bible says, "Wives, submit yourselves to your own husbands as you do to the Lord. For the husband is the head of the wife as Christ is the head of the church, his body, of which he is the Savior. Now as the church submits to Christ, so also wives should submit to their husbands in everything" (Ephesians 5:22–24). This is obviously an unpopular passage today, but what are we supposed to do with biblical statements like this—delete or ignore them? Surely not; they are God's Word. Some Christians explain away the countercultural message of this verse, making it less abrasive. So what do we make of this?

We should recognize that it doesn't mean that women are supposed to be servants to men or always agree with them. It is focused on the marriage relationship, not every woman-man interaction. These verses are focused on order and peace in the home, and anchoring our relationships at home with Christ's love for his people (the church). The apostle Paul continues by saying, "Husbands, love your wives, just as Christ loved the church and gave himself up for her" (v. 25). God has called husbands to lead the same way Christ leads his church: with such selfless love that he lays down his life for her. Jesus did not wait passively to provide for his church, and he didn't show up on earth to boss people around. Instead, he said, "The Son of Man did not come to be served, but to serve, and to give his life as a ransom for many" (Matthew 20:28). That is the type of leadership men are called to in the home.

This teaching has been abused by some individuals and churches who emphasize the "wives should submit to their husbands in everything" part of Ephesians 5:24. Sometimes I think it's helpful to understand verses like this by imagining the exact opposite. What would a marriage look like if a husband and wife competed with each other? Every decision would become a matter for division and conflict. That would be terrible! Instead, God's design is for a husband and wife to lovingly seek genuine unity and agreement, with a posture to lay aside their self-interest and to trust each other. When a disagreement still remains and someone needs to submit, this verse indicates that the responsibility and accountability fall on the husband's leadership over the home. If a husband is leading his family according to Scripture, this type of situation will be very rare and handled with great care and caution.

So, to summarize: Men and women are equally created in the image of God, both are called to live according to God's creation mandate (Genesis 1:28), and husbands and wives are to love one another and to put each other's needs first. They shouldn't look at one another with competition or the desire to boss the other around. Yes, the husband is called to lead, but he is also held accountable before God for such leadership. However, this doesn't mean the wife is a mindless servant.

Unfortunately, this message has been twisted in countless ways, making it that much more important to clarify why the Bible would say this about husbands and wives. (Spoiler alert: It's because of what marriage represents!)

WHAT MARRIAGE REPRESENTS

If we are going to be faithful icons of God, we need to have a biblical theology of sex and marriage because they show us what God's personal and intimate love for us looks like. So when your friends and peers are treating sex and porn like it's no big deal, you have an opportunity to embrace the holy call of God to be "set apart" as different. I know it can sound weird, and that's okay, but God's love satisfies the human soul in ways that no man or woman ever could.

Christians care about guarding the dignity of marriage between a man and a woman because marriage is a theological symbol of the gospel. Rejecting biblical sexuality is a rejection of God's good creation. We aren't trying to ruin anyone's fun or point an arrogant finger at others to tell them what they should be doing. It would be so much easier to stay silent and avoid disagreements. But we are willing to have these difficult and awkward conversations because we truly believe that God's Word teaches what is best for God's image-bearers, and openly embracing sin is not ultimately fulfilling for anyone.

The Bible's teachings about gender and sexuality flow from the foundational human relationship: marriage. This means we need to begin at the beginning. Genesis 1 and 2 emphasize that God created male and female in his image. Scripture describes marriage as a "one flesh" relationship (Genesis 2:24; more on this in a minute). Many LGBTQ+-affirming people assume that Christians are anti-gay because they're bigots or think homosexuality is weird or gross. Sadly, that's probably true for some Christians, but this assumption completely misunderstands the Bible's objections to homosexuality. If you want to really understand what the Bible teaches about homosexuality, you need to understand what the Bible promotes before digging into what it prohibits.

Marriage is one of the clearest ways people can be iconic of God. He created Eve, the first woman, from Adam's rib. This is something easily overlooked, but it's significant. God didn't grab a handful of dust to create Eve from scratch, like he did with Adam (Genesis 2:7). Neither did he create Eve from Adam's head to make her his superior, nor from his foot to make her his servant. God created her from his rib so that she would be his "helper" (Genesis 2:18). The Hebrew word that's translated as "helper" isn't an insult or demeaning, even though it can appear that way to modern readers. It's a unique Hebrew word that has to do with a partner who helps you claim victory. No one would look down upon or belittle the role of reinforcements who came in to help you win a battle. That is why, after describing the creation of Eve, Genesis 2:24 concludes, "That is why a man leaves his father and mother and is united to his wife, and they become one flesh." The message is that Adam simply could not succeed in his mission without Eve's reinforcement.

Men and women need each other to bear God's image well. This is evident even in the way male and female bodies were created to become "one flesh" in order to create new life. This was God's design for humanity to fulfill his calling in the creation mandate of Genesis 1:28: to "be fruitful and increase in number; fill the earth and subdue it." We depend on each other and cannot reproduce alone. We do this as one flesh. There is honor and dignity for both partners in creating and raising future generations of image-bearers.

Biblical marriage is a covenant (that's the strongest type of formal agreement between two people) between a man and a woman. The New Testament later explains that the faithful, intimate love between husband and wife shines a spotlight on the way Christ Jesus loves his church (Ephesians 5:32). The two people involved are different but complementary—just as Christ and the Christian are different. This was always God's intent for marriage, going all the way back to creation! Marriage is an earthly image of the heavenly reality. In this biblical metaphor, Christ is the husband and Christians are the wife. The big picture of the Bible's message about marriage is that it represents God's intimacy with his image-bearers, and this message is conveyed through the union of two different but complementary lovers coming together in the covenant of marriage.

This is why same-sex marriages cannot be considered biblical marriage: They literally cannot represent Christ and the church, which is the theological meaning of marriage in the first place. The Bible expands on this theological symbolism by equating adultery with idolatry (and vice versa). When a husband or wife is unfaithful to their covenant partner by giving their intimate affections to someone else, it symbolizes spiritual idolatry, just like Scripture often equates ancient Israel's worship of false gods to spiritual adultery (see Jeremiah 3; Ezekiel 16; Hosea 1:2). Sleeping around and having sex outside of marriage is equated with a type of spiritual looseness, because you are giving yourself intimately to someone you are not in covenant with (Ezekiel 6:9; James 4:4–5). This is why Romans 1:18–27 references homosexuality as evidence that people have begun to worship themselves and other created things, rather than the true God. These statements are not merely cultural judgments. They are theological statements that flow from the Bible's teaching about what marriage is: a representation of God's intimate union with his image-bearers.

Sexuality and gender and relationships are all part of God's created order. This is why we need to remember what we are as human beings in order to discover who we are as men and women.

DOES YOUR GENDER MATTER?

Some people will tell you that your gender is a social construct and that men and women are exactly the same in God's eyes. While I fully and joyfully agree that men and women equally bear God's image and are equally loved by him, I also think it's fairly obvious we are not the same. From our genetic coding to our body structures and a female's exclusive ability to conceive and give birth, men and women are not the same. Our differences don't need to create a battle of the sexes to determine which is superior, but neither should they be overlooked or minimized. God created us differently, but in ways that complete and strengthen each other.

For example, I took a break while writing this chapter to bring my teenage daughter to a volleyball game. The opposing team was the only co-ed team in the league, comprised of mostly girls and two boys. Those boys served and hit the ball noticeably harder than anyone else on the court, even though neither of them were big or muscular. League rules limit boys to playing in the back line because their spikes and hits from the front row could injure the girls on the other team. The natural physical differences between the boys and girls are obvious to any honest observer.

I know this is a highly sensitive issue and I'm sympathetic to readers who are intersex (born with both male and female sex organs), who personally struggle with gender dysphoria, or who love those who do. Today's conversations about gender identity separate a person's sex (their biological identity) and their gender (how they understand their masculinity or femininity). But separating these as two independent realities rejects and undermines the Bible's teaching about what it means to be a human being who is created in God's image. This message can create uncomfortable and tense conversations today, but that doesn't change the Bible's message about what it means to be a human being. The Bible's teaching about personhood encompasses the whole person: the body and soul are united.

Gender is a core aspect of what it means to be human. This is why transgender ideology is so deceiving: It radically redefines what it means to be a human being according to one's self-understanding. It separates a person's "true self" from their physical body by expressing that their gender identity and physical body are not in alignment, and so the body should be brought into conformity with their gender identity. This is so troubling because it undermines God's declaration that his creation of male and female is "very good" (Genesis 1:31).

How do we make sense of gender dysphoria and same-sex attraction and intersex individuals? Again, we look to God's creation and what went wrong with it. Everything in creation has been tainted by the curse of sin, including nature, our bodies, mental health, sexuality, and gender. In this way, sin is at the root of all sorts of struggles we experience. This is not always willful sin that we have committed. But the effects of sin's curse stretch out into all creation. Not everything that seems to happen naturally is therefore good or right, because even our desires have been twisted from their created order. This doesn't lead Christians to harshly dismiss or criticize those who are struggling with their gender or sexuality; rather, it invites us to follow Jesus's example of compassion.

The story about Jesus and the blind man in John 9 is a good example.

As he went along, he saw a man blind from birth. His disciples asked him, "Rabbi, who sinned, this man or his parents, that he was born blind?" "Neither this man nor his parents sinned," said Jesus, "but this happened so that the works of God might be displayed in him." (vv. 1–3)

Similar to this man who was born blind, those who are born with a disability, mental illness, gender dysphoria, or as an intersex person are called to walk a difficult path. We should not assume it's a punishment for sin they or their parents have committed. The biological causes of their challenges might be debatable and complicated, but their life mission remains the same as everyone else's: to live as icons who display the nature and character of God. This hardship is one way that God displays his faithfulness and sufficiency through them.

The Bible's message about gender and sexuality is holy and good, so we cannot simply dismiss the biblical teaching as outdated because it's become unpopular or because we want to be accepting of our friends. We should be patient and compassionate toward those who struggle with their sexuality or gender identity, even as we seek to help them bear God's image faithfully.

RESPONDING TO LGBTQ CHALLENGES THAT QUESTION THE IMAGE OF GOD

Although this chapter has already addressed some of these questions from a biblical and theological viewpoint,

I want to offer some practical counsel about how to respond to LGBTQ+ challenges that are raised in your normal interactions with friends and peers.

Although homosexuality is contrary to God's intent for his icons, many who are living with same-sex attraction simply feel that it is more natural than heterosexual desire. Similarly, some people recall gender confusion from a very young age. As we've already seen, these are difficult realities in a world that has been fractured by the curse of sin. The experiences of same-sex attraction and gender confusion do not confirm their goodness or holiness any more than the experiences of anger or lust make them good or holy. In a similar way that unmarried, heterosexual Christians are called to resist their sexual desires, those who experience homosexual desires are also called to resist sinful temptations in order to live with sexual holiness.

The rise of teenagers experiencing gender dysphoria is skyrocketing and has been referred to as a "social contagion."[1] This is a fancy phrase that means it becomes more common among individuals as it becomes more common within the group. The more LGBTQ+ friends someone has, the more likely they will begin to experience LGBTQ+ feelings. This isn't meant to belittle an adolescent's experience, but it is an acknowledgment that there are significant social factors that encourage gender confusion, oftentimes without people being aware that's what's happening. Because we are social people who are built for relationships, we should pray that our lives will have an impact on those around us. Perhaps your iconic faithfulness will enable you to show them the glory and goodness of God.

When I think about the best way to faithfully respond to these young men and women whom I love, I often think about Jesus's interaction with the woman who was dragged before him for judgment in John 8:1–11. She was caught in the act of adultery and brought before Jesus by the Pharisees for judgment. They said to Jesus, "Teacher, this woman was caught in the act of adultery. In the Law Moses commanded us to stone such women. Now what do you say?" (vv. 4–5).

Was she guilty of sin? Yes, she was. Did the Law of Moses provide for the judgment they said? Yes, it did. But did the Pharisees actually care about this woman or God's justice? No, they didn't because they only brought the woman and not the man. Jesus saw through their trap and had mercy on her. But he did not affirm her sinful behavior. Instead, he said to her, "Go now and leave your life of sin" (v. 11).

I believe this is the best example for how Christians can be iconic in today's culture. We must not call good what God has called sinful. We also should not follow the Pharisees' example of singling out one type of sexual sinner while overlooking the need for others to also repent. We need to receive and reflect the grace and mercy of God that was put on display through Jesus Christ. This means we refuse to allow someone's sexuality to be the most important thing about them, and it means that we call them toward the goodness of what God has intended for them to experience. There's a lot of wisdom and patience needed here, but when we are icons of God in this confused world, we will show mercy to sinners—even as we invite them to leave their life of sin behind and follow Jesus.

GOSPEL CLARITY: BECOMING ICONIC MEN AND WOMEN

Because this book is for teenagers and young adults, it's safe to say that you are likely not married. So why did I take up so many pages talking about the meaning of marriage instead of focusing on issues that you're experiencing today?

The Bible's message about the image of God drives the way we think about gender and sexuality, which is one of the most divisive issues in our culture today. Too many messages about LGBTQ+ issues fail to start at the beginning or paint a bigger picture about why the Bible prohibits homosexuality and transgender identities. If we try having conversations about sexuality without anchoring those conversations in what it means to be a human being, then we're building on a sandy foundation instead of on the rock (see Matthew 7:24–27). We believe that sexuality and gender get to the heart of what it means to be a human being who is created in the image of God.

Additionally, the way you think about marriage sets the tone for how you think about sexual holiness and intimacy. And that affects the way you think about singleness, dating, and relationships. If marriage is just a piece of paper, then sure, treat relationships casually, sleep around, and live with whomever you want. But if marriage is a holy representation of God's love for his people to experience true intimacy, and if we want to be faithful icons of Christ in this world, then we need to take marriage and sexuality seriously.

We all crave intimacy: to be fully known and fully loved. Sex doesn't create intimacy; it's an expression of it. Sex is a way for a husband and wife to affirm their full and complete acceptance of one another. But so many people today treat sex like it's a shortcut toward intimacy or as just another way to have a good time. God wants so much more for you than that. Our sexuality is an expression of the intimacy we were created to enjoy in God as his image-bearers. This is why true intimacy isn't found through sex and marriage, but through embracing your identity as God's icon in your world.

If we want to find wholeness and freedom and peace, then we need Jesus more than anything else. Whatever types of relational pain and sexual temptations you endure, Jesus is the "living water" (John 4:10–14) who satisfies completely. By faith in Christ, we receive the indwelling of the Holy Spirit, who brings us into the very heart of God. The Holy Spirit also adopts us into a spiritual family. When we walk in faith, we are walking alongside brothers and sisters in Christ who strengthen us when we are weak. One of God's greatest blessings is that none of us has to walk alone—the focus of our next chapter.

QUESTIONS FOR REFLECTION

1. Have you ever thought about sexual and gender identity as topics that are grounded in our humanity? How does our identity as image-bearers bring greater clarity to these confusing topics?

2. Does a biblical view of marriage shape the way you approach relationships today? How can this

perspective help you navigate dating relationships prior to marriage?

3. Do you believe that God's will for your sexuality and gender is to promote wholeness and joy, not to limit your pleasure or happiness? Why can that be hard to embrace?

Chapter 3
Iconic Community

Mia was spiritually curious and started coming to youth group with a longtime friend. Church was new to her and she was interested in the messages, but Mia struggled with the hypocrisy she saw in the other students who acted like Christians at church but lived very un-Christian lives the rest of the week. Even worse, she kept hearing on social media about Christian leaders getting exposed as hypocrites. Although the Bible seemed appealing to her, it also seemed like Christians hardly even believed it was true.

Sometimes well-intentioned Christians reply to the Mias in their lives by saying things like, "We're all sinners saved by grace," or "Judge Christianity by Christ, not by Christians." These are true statements. But we need to acknowledge that the public witness of Christians is important. Yes, who you are matters. Who *we* are matters too. If Christians—especially Christian leaders—act like they don't believe their own message, then why should anyone *become* a Christian at all? This is a legitimate issue for people like Mia, and we shouldn't minimize their confusion.

One aspect of what it means to be created in the image of God that's easily overlooked is our corporate image: who we are as the people of God and how we bear God's image together. Many of us can read the earlier chapters as a personal call to holiness and faithfulness, and rightly so. But it's also a call to holiness and faithfulness for the corporate church because we bear the image of God together, and the world is watching.

AN ICONIC PEOPLE: ISRAEL AS THE PEOPLE OF GOD

Biblically speaking, if you are a Christian then your participation in the family of God began in the Old Testament, is secured through the New Testament, and is applied today. This is why it's important to understand the role of ancient Israel and how the gospel invites all nations into the family of God. Living an iconic life isn't just about you, individually. Being God's image in your world is also about who Christians are, corporately, as the people of God.

God's covenant family started with Abraham, continued through Isaac, and eventually led to the establishment of Israel. The Lord made covenants with Israel through Abraham (Genesis 15), Moses (Exodus 19–24), and David (2 Samuel 7). These covenants set the terms of their unique relationship as God's chosen people. Israel was unique and special among all the other nations who were not God's covenant people. But the prophet Isaiah reminded Israel that God's intent was always to make them an iconic "light for the nations" (Isaiah 49:6 ESV) You see, God's intent was to restore Israel in the image of God as a nation in order that all nations would see the glory and goodness of God in them, both individually and as a people.

This is God's intent with the church too. This becomes very clear by understanding the significance of Pentecost. When Jesus proclaimed himself to be the "light of the world" (John 8:12), and when the Holy Spirit fell upon the Christians on Pentecost (Acts 2:1–4), guess what happened: The believers started speaking in languages they didn't even know. Pentecost was one of the biggest pilgrim holidays of the Jewish year, so Israel was full of faithful Jewish men and women who lived in distant countries and spoke different languages. By inspiring the apostles to proclaim the good news of Jesus's life, death, resurrection, and coming return, the Holy Spirit was flinging open the doors to the family of God. God's people are a multi-ethnic family.

Ultimately, Israel forgot what they were: icons of God's adoptive love to the nations. Their desire to maintain a distinct identity as God's chosen people ironically led them to overlook the bigger picture about why God called them in the first place. Christians can be tempted similarly to lose sight of our image-bearing witness to the world. That's why it's so important for us to remember Moses's message to Israel as they renewed their covenant with the Lord in Deuteronomy. He told them,

> For you are a people holy to the Lord your God. The Lord your God has chosen you out of all the peoples on the face of the earth to be his people, his treasured possession. The Lord did not set his affection on you and choose you because you

> were more numerous than other peoples, for you were the fewest of all peoples. But it was because the LORD loved you and kept the oath he swore to your ancestors that he brought you out with a mighty hand and redeemed you from the land of slavery, from the power of Pharaoh king of Egypt. (Deuteronomy 7:6–8)

God has always called and adopted his children purely out of his own gracious love.

Their obedience—then and now—was always meant to be an obedience that flows from confidence in God's saving love, and God intended for that faithfulness to be a public image for the nations to behold what kind of God they worshipped. An iconic community involves the faithfulness of individuals and the community at large—and this is greatly influenced by the community's leaders.

ICONIC LEADERSHIP: KING SAUL AND DAVID AS GOD'S IMAGE-BEARERS

Leadership is inherently iconic. This is why leadership isn't about power (forcing others to do what you want) but servanthood (leading according to what's best for the people). Godly leaders view themselves as icons of God's sovereign reign. They know their authority is borrowed, not permanent. Godly authorities show us the glory and goodness of God, while wicked authorities make us yearn for God's kingdom to come. The most natural place to see this in Scripture is in the kings of Israel.

Kings filled a few important roles. First and most obviously, they wielded power and authority to make important decisions, levy taxes, and create laws. Second, as the leader of their nation, they also represented their people to others. This is why defeated kings used to be publicly humiliated or tortured by conquering armies, in order to tell the people, "If we can do this to your king, we can do this to you!" Third, by the nature of their leadership and authority, they represented God's reign to the people. This is why the godliness and integrity of the king's personal life was significant.

Israel wasn't supposed to simply be a great nation, they were called to be iconic of God before all nations. Accordingly, Israel's king was to lead the people in godliness and holiness. Perhaps the most obvious contrast of godly and ungodly leadership comes by comparing King Saul and King David.

Israel did not have a king for hundreds of years. Instead, they were led by the judges and prophets whom God provided. Eventually, the people grew jealous of the other nations who had royalty. Saul was anointed as Israel's first king after they begged and pleaded for God to provide one so they could be like the other nations. Saul was tall, strong, and handsome—all the external qualities you would look for in a leader. But he lacked character and integrity. We see his lack of character most clearly in his preparation for battle against the Philistines.

The armies were gathered and Saul was in trouble. Samuel the prophet said he would come and give instructions from the Lord, but he didn't arrive when Saul expected him. Instead of waiting for the prophet, Saul took matters into his own hands. Because Saul impatiently doubted God, Samuel rebuked him harshly when he arrived (1 Samuel 13:13–14). Whereas faithfulness would have established Saul's reign, his impatience and faithlessness meant he would not only lose this battle against the Philistines, but he would also be stripped of his kingly authority. Samuel declared that God would replace him with a "man after his own heart" (1 Samuel 13:14).

God's judgment on Saul for his lack of faith might seem harsh to us, but remember, Saul was Israel's first king. As the king, he held incredible power—politically and spiritually. He was supposed to be a representative of the Lord to the people. But he doesn't respond to this prophetic rebuke with humility or repentance. Instead, this judgment only enrages Saul further, sending him into a tailspin of arrogance and rage that continues until his death on the battlefield in 1 Samuel 31.

By contrast, we meet David as Samuel is searching for this "man after God's own heart." While Samuel is sulking over Saul's failures, God sends him to Bethlehem to anoint one of Jesse's sons as the new king. Although Samuel is impressed with David's oldest brother, Eliab, the Lord says, "Do not consider his appearance or his height, for I have rejected him. The LORD does not look at the things people look at. People look at the outward appearance, but the LORD looks at the heart" (1 Samuel 16:7). One by one, God rejects all of Jesse's seven oldest sons.

It's interesting how David's older brothers are all described similarly as Saul: tall, strong, and impressive. David, however, was young and unimpressive, and no one had high expectations for him. He wasn't even brought to Samuel for consideration until all the others were rejected. There's a clear message about what it means to be iconic: It's about the heart.

David's reign as king is far from perfect. We read about his sin against Bathsheba and the murder of her husband as an attempt to cover up his sin, among other regrettable actions. Yet the biggest difference between Saul and David were the spiritual states of their hearts. When Saul was confronted by Samuel, Saul doubled down on his sin and took matters into his own hands. However, when David was confronted by the prophet Nathan, he confessed his sin to the Lord and repented.

This is the backstory behind Psalm 51, which was written by David and begins,

> Have mercy on me, O God,
> according to your unfailing love;
> according to your great compassion
> blot out my transgressions.
> Wash away all my iniquity
> and cleanse me from my sin.
> For I know my transgressions,
> and my sin is always before me. (vv. 1–3)

David wasn't a man after God's own heart because he was sinless, but because he recognized his need for God's mercy and provision.

Both Saul and David came from places of unimportance and were given a significant role: king of Israel. Incredible! Neither of them could have ever imagined such a thing would happen to them. This wasn't merely an opportunity to grow wealthy and powerful, but to be the leader and representative of God's chosen people.

Saul received his kingship, used it for his own glory, and was thus removed. David received it with humility and sought to please the Lord. This doesn't mean Saul was completely evil and David was completely righteous. But when they were confronted with their sin, their responses couldn't be more opposite, and that made all the difference.

It's easy for us to compare Saul and David and identify ourselves with David. We all want to identify with the person who did things right. But if I'm honest, I most identify with Israel and their desire to conform to those around them.

CONFORMITY: RESISTING THAT OLD TEMPTATION

God's people haven't changed that much, have they? We still want to find ways to be God's people while trying to live like those around us. Whether it's compromising on the language we use with friends, the clothes we wear, the music we listen to, or our beliefs about gender and sexuality, we aren't the first ones to wrestle with the questions, *Is my faith worth the sacrifice? Is God worth it?* Conformity isn't a new temptation for God's people.

The church's identity is rooted in Israel's calling. As we've already seen, our Christian roots are Jewish roots. Whether you have any Jewish heritage or not, every Christian is a child of Abraham and has been "grafted" into the root of God's promise to Israel (Romans 11:17). Israel's calling to be representatives of the Lord before all the nations of the world is our calling too. This is most clearly seen in Jesus's own words to his disciples when he taught,

"You are the light of the world. A town built on a hill cannot be hidden. Neither do people light a lamp and put it under a bowl. Instead they put it on its stand, and it gives light to everyone in the house. In the same way, let your light shine before others, that they may see your good deeds and glorify your Father in heaven." (Matthew 5:14–16)

If we are going to be lights in the world, then we need to remember that means we're different from the world. Here are three areas in which Christians collectively need God-given courage to live as faithful icons today.

Courage to be different

One of the most difficult challenges of being and bearing God's image in your world is how noticeably different you are from those around you. Sometimes I hear other youth pastors talk about how they want unbelievers to come to their youth group and see that "Christians are normal people, just like everyone else." I get it. We don't want to give the impression that Christians are unrelatable weirdos. But I hope the students who come to my youth group experience something they don't see in their school cafeteria or in the hallways. I hope the way we play games and handle winning and losing is different from what happens in gym class or on the sports field. I hope the way we handle disruptions and disagreements during small groups is different from the way some teachers handle it in their public school.

I hope the atmosphere of our group is unashamedly and obviously shaped by the gospel of Jesus Christ and that it stands out as beautifully different.

Christians are called to stand out and be different. This is true of us as followers (remember Israel's desire to be like the other nations around them) and as leaders (we are called to represent the Lord faithfully). If we are called to be the light of the world yet don't want to stand out as different, then we're going to hide the light of Christ or put it on a dimmer switch. Light shines in the darkness. Are we willing to bear God's light in our world?

Courage to remember our unity

When you feel like you're the only Christian around, it's encouraging to remember the beautiful diversity of Christian fellowship. Fellowship isn't just another word for hanging out together. Think about a gathering of like-minded people who are different from each other but have a shared core identity and a shared mission, so they're working in harmony together to fulfill their common purpose. Now, infuse that shared harmony with encouragement among the group members to be and bear God's image. That's what Christian fellowship is all about.

Even though you might feel like you're the only Christian around, you probably aren't. Every Christian is part of God's big family called "the church," which transcends ethnicity and culture and even time. We share a common identity with brothers and sisters in Christ from every country in the world. It's so easy for us to become completely immersed in our own tightknit

Christian communities that we think our experience is representative of the whole. But that's not true. Maybe you feel like there aren't any other Christians in your area because you're only looking to people from your own culture or background. But when you open your eyes to celebrate what Christ is doing within the broader church, you'll find a whole new Christian community you didn't even know existed.

A valuable part of remembering your unity with other believers is your unity with Christians around the world who are experiencing great persecution and suffering for their faith. We can pray for them and make their needs known to those who are unaware of their suffering, even as these dear brothers and sisters in the faith can encourage us to stay faithful. If they can endure such hardships and painful suffering while remaining faithful, then we can share in their suffering by enduring our own hardships. Remembering our unity with the persecuted church gives us courage to endure our own hardships in a way that honors God.

Courage to live with integrity

Integrity is a common-enough word that we should all understand what it means. But we don't. Living with integrity means that we are the same person in every setting: with school friends, on the soccer field, playing video games online, and when we're alone. What would happen if someone filmed sixty-second videos of you at randomly selected points of the day—every day for a month? Would there be multiple versions of you on display, depending on who else is around or what you're doing? Or would there be one consistent life on display that honors the Lord and is appropriate for each situation? Courageously praying for integrity leads us to ask, *Am I the same person whether I'm at church, at home, or with different groups of friends?*

Our world tells us that results are what matter. The more you do, the more you're worth. If you have to step over a few people on your way to the top, then that's what you need to do. But that's not a Christian message. If we believe our worth is determined by our accomplishments or by other's opinions of us, then we'll never live with Christian integrity because we'll be a different person depending on whoever is around us. The gospel frees from other peoples' opinions of us. We don't live for the applause of others (although it's still nice to be affirmed!). Now we're able to become who God made us to be without worrying about impressing others, because we know that our value and worth is secure in God. The courage to live with Christian integrity comes from our confidence in God's faithfulness and steadfast love.

Who you are individually matters. And who we are as a Christian community matters. As gospel-shaped people, one important way we represent the Lord to an onlooking world is the way we confess our sin and repent when we fail. So if you've given into pressure to conform to the world around you, then take this moment to admit where you've sinned and ask the Lord to conform you to the image of Christ instead. Let this be an encouragement for each of us to serve the Lord with integrity because we represent him to others who are watching. We are icons of Christ. It's not just what we do; it's who we are.

GOSPEL CLARITY: ICONIC TOGETHER

No Christian is ever alone. Sure, we might feel lonely on occasion. But every Christian has been adopted into the people of God, is united with Christ by faith, and is being prayed for by Christ in glory. That means you don't need to try to be iconic in your world alone. Find a faithful church and get connected—because you need them, and they need you.

The reality is, none of us can do this alone. Even King David, who was a man after God's own heart, fell into serious sin and needed to be called out. We need people who love us enough to point out our sin, and who love Jesus enough to remind us about his restoring grace. We are iconic together—not because we're awesome or self-righteous, but because Christ forgives sinners, clothes them in his righteousness, and forms them into a spiritual family.

As you continue to read this book and apply its message to your life, remember that it's not only about who you are individually, but also about who we are, together.

QUESTIONS FOR REFLECTION

1. Why is it so tempting for us to only think about being and bearing God's image as individuals? Why is it important for us to remember our corporate identity?
2. What are some common struggles or challenges that can harm Christians' corporate witness in our world?
3. How do you think Christians can be a better public witness in our world today? What's one area where you'd like to see us more faithfully reflect Christ?

Chapter 4
Iconic Prayer

A G. I. Joe action figure tested my faith when I was a kid. My Sunday school teacher taught the class that God would answer our prayers that are offered in Jesus's name. I believed her, so for the month before Christmas, I faithfully prayed for a G. I. Joe action figure set (it was an enemy tank with missiles piloted by Cobra Commander—sweet!). I was utterly devastated when Christmas arrived and there was no tank.

I know that's a silly story, but it was a big deal for me as a kid, because it's not just about me wanting a tank. My confidence in prayer was genuinely shaken because it made me wonder if God really listens to and answers prayer. It's easy for me to look back today and shake my head, saying, *Mike, that's not what it means to pray in Jesus's name*, but there's a significant spiritual issue at stake here. Honestly, I think many of us are guilty of praying those simplistic tank prayers, then feeling confusion or resentment when they aren't answered the way we hoped. *God, help me pass this test. God, heal my grandmother. God, help me find a boyfriend/girlfriend.* When the answer is no, we're shaken. And what about the times when these "failed prayers" lead to real difficulty or suffering in life?

If faith is the string that unites people and God, then prayer is the act of strumming the string of faith to make it sing with music. As a child, I thought the only way to pluck the strings of prayer was to make requests of God. But that's like thinking you can only play one type of song on a guitar. Just as there are happy songs, sad songs, and love songs, there are different types of prayer too. The Psalms are like a diverse playlist of prayers to God; they don't all sound the same.

When we stop plucking the string of prayer, our relationship with God often begins to grow lukewarm. When our prayers are cold, distant, and impersonal, that's a sign that there's something unhealthy in our affection for God. Understanding what prayer is and how to pray various kinds of prayers will help you rekindle your love for God so you can bear his image with joy, even when life is hard.

PSALMS: THE PRAYER BOOK OF THE BIBLE

When I was a teenager, I thought all psalms were like Psalm 23—poems about how nice and sweet God is and how I should just love him so much—or songs of praise that people turned into songs we'd sing on Sunday mornings. Aside from those two types of psalms, I honestly didn't think much about them. Imagine my surprise when I discovered there are many different types of psalms! This makes sense, because the book of Psalms is the prayer book of the Bible, and people pray different types of prayers depending on what's happening in life at the moment. And as the prayer book of the Bible, the Psalms also guided the nation of Israel as the people kept their covenant to the Lord.

We are called to reflect God's glory and goodness in our world whether life is hard or full of blessing. But how do we do that if we only know how to ask God for things and sing happy praise songs? The different types of psalms can help us learn how to pray in every circumstance.

Psalms of thanksgiving and supplication

Our need and gratitude should flow together in prayer. This is why I think it's helpful to lump thankfulness and supplication together, because one is the request (*supplication* is a fancy word that has to do with asking God to "supply" you with what you're asking for) while the other is an expression of thankfulness for God's provision. They often coexist within the same psalm, either because the psalmist is bringing a request to God with thankful confidence that he will answer, or because he's expressing praise and thanksgiving for the ways God has blessed him. Psalms 7 and 30 present good examples of asking God for deliverance, then thanking him for it.

> Lord my God, I take refuge in you;
>   save and deliver me from all who pursue me,
>   or they will tear me apart like a lion
>   and rip me to pieces with no one to rescue
>   me. . . .
> I will give thanks to the Lord because of his
>   righteousness;

I will sing the praises of the name of the Lord
   Most High. (Psalm 7:1–2, 17)

I will exalt you, Lord,
for you lifted me out of the depths
and did not let my enemies gloat over me.
Lord my God, I called to you for help,
and you healed me.
You, Lord, brought me up from the realm of
   the dead;
you spared me from going down to the pit.
   (Psalm 30:1–3)

It's impossible to live an iconic life that honors God if you lack a thankful heart. Some people walk around as if they can only see the negatives, the struggles, and the things they do not have. This is a victim mindset that seems to highlight the ways God and the world have let them down. If you live this way, then you have been blinded to the countless blessings God has already given you, and you're likely struggling to live with joyful faith that he will provide for your daily life. Your prayers will be full of supplication and sorely lacking in thanksgiving.

Let's be clear: It's good and healthy to bring your prayer requests to God. Don't feel guilty or like an immature Christian for asking God to help you with your exams, give you wisdom about how to deal with difficult relationships, or provide you with a good job upon graduation. These are stressful situations, and God cares for you. Jesus says that God cares for you so much, he even knows how many hairs are on your head (Luke 12:7). God delights in giving good gifts to his children who pray (Matthew 7:11). But if this is the only type of prayer you offer, then perhaps you view God like a cosmic vending machine more than as a Father who cares and provides for you.

Gratitude will radically shift the way you pray when you're in need because God isn't someone you need to bargain with or persuade—he is your Father in heaven who delights in taking care of his children. Imagine the way it would change your life to regularly bring your requests to God, not as someone presenting a shopping list but as a son or daughter asking their heavenly Father for help. Then imagine how it would change your view of God to come to him with regular prayers of thanksgiving, remembering all the ways he has blessed and cared for you. Prayers of thanksgiving and supplication naturally lead us to praise.

Psalms of praise

If you hear a psalm read during a worship service or if it's included in a song, then it's probably a psalm of praise. That's because they are joyful expressions of adoration and worship to God.

Even though we tend to equate worship with singing, they aren't the same thing. Music can be a powerful way to express worship, but prayer is also a worshipful expression of praise. Sometimes these psalms of praise are lofty and extravagant, while others are relational expressions of affection for God. Still others are intended for corporate worship. Consider the following examples:

> Lord, our Lord, how majestic is your name in all the earth! (Psalm 8:1)

The Lord is my shepherd, I lack nothing.
He makes me lie down in green pastures.
(Psalm 23:1–2)

Every day I will praise you
and extol your name for ever and ever.
Great is the Lord and most worthy of praise;
his greatness no one can fathom.
(Psalm 145:2–3)

These psalms of praise lead us in worship and remind us who God is. He is the One we worship, so the emphasis isn't about us and our feelings, but about him and what he has done.

Many Christian songs today that are sung in worship aren't "worship" songs, but songs of thanksgiving because their emphasis is about our experience and response to God. Think about your favorite worship songs and the ways you praise God in prayer. Do you praise him for who he is, or for what he does for you? Songs of thanksgiving for God's faithfulness and kindness to us are important, but the psalms of praise show us what it looks like to worship God simply because he is worthy.

This is why it's so important for every Christian to study the holiness and nature of God. God is holy and mysterious. We will never fully understand him because he is so much more glorious than we could ever fathom; yet he has revealed himself as our heavenly Father. If we are going to live as faithful icons who display God's character and tell others about his saving work, then it's good for us to spend regular time in these psalms of praise. As we do, we should celebrate that he is worthy of our worship because of who he is, not merely because of what he's done for us.

Psalms of lament

Praise in times of suffering, however, often sounds like a lament. Sometimes we can feel like we need to put on a happy face when we pray, even if life is confusing, complicated, or painful. But we don't need to do this. We can always bring our genuine selves before the Lord in prayer. God can handle strong and raw emotions.

This is where the psalms of lament are really helpful. These are prayers where the psalm writer is mourning, suffering, or in danger. Sometimes, he feels like God has forgotten him. These psalms are biblical reminders that God accepts even the unhappy prayers of his children. Here are a few examples:

> How long, Lord? Will you forget me forever?
> How long will you hide your face from me?
>   (Psalm 13:1)

> Help, Lord, for no one is faithful anymore;
> those who are loyal have vanished from the
>   human race.
> Everyone lies to their neighbor;
> they flatter with their lips
> but harbor deception in their hearts.
>   (Psalm 12:1–2)

O God, why have you rejected us forever?
Why does your anger smolder against the
   sheep of your pasture?
(Psalm 74:1)

The verses above are good snapshots, but it might be helpful for you to take a minute to choose one and read the full psalm. The writer is completely honest about his situation, yet he casts himself before God for help. Think about it: If he truly believed that God wouldn't listen or had actually forgotten him, then he wouldn't be praying. Psalms of lament show us that faithful people have always struggled with seasons of deep grief and conflicted emotions—and they were found faithful because they kept seeking the Lord in prayer anyway.

When you pray in the midst of hardship, you're practicing your faith more than you probably realize. Think about how much faith it requires to pray when you really don't want to! It takes a lot of faith to trust God when your heart and emotions aren't feeling it. In those seasons, we lay aside our feelings and fears that try persuading us that God has forgotten us, and we choose to trust God's promise instead.

When you're feeling this way, it might be best to pray your prayers of lament with another believer who can strengthen and support you. When we do that, we become living icons of faith, showing that our confidence and security are in who God is and what he's promised, rather than in what we can see or feel today. Such confidence in God sets us free to remember God's glory and goodness in every circumstance.

Psalms of confession

There's a common saying that's proven true in my own life: "The Bible will keep you from sin, or sin will keep you from the Bible." This principle is true about prayer too. Prayer isn't a magical incantation that protects us from temptation. But when you develop a healthy prayer life, it redirects your desires away from sin and toward intimacy with your Father in heaven.

Sometimes we can feel so convicted by our sin that it becomes difficult to pray. This can even happen when we remember God's rich mercy but prayer simply feels impossible. When this happens, the conviction of sin is keeping us from the very thing that removes its burden, and then we fall deeper into sin's grasp.

It might be helpful to build on the previous chapter's example of David's faithfulness as a "man after God's own heart." His sexual sin and abuse of power are also well-known. He stayed home in his palace when he should've been leading his army. When he saw Bathsheba's beauty, he commanded her to come to the palace to sleep with him even though she was married to one of his officers, whom he effectually had murdered later on the battlefield. After multiple cover-up attempts, his sin was brought into the light. David wrote Psalm 51 as an expression of deep sorrow and confession. Here's how the psalm begins:

> Have mercy on me, O God,
> according to your unfailing love;
> according to your great compassion
> blot out my transgressions.

Wash away all my iniquity
and cleanse me from my sin.
For I know my transgressions,
and my sin is always before me. (vv. 1–3)

When David confessed his sin, he didn't make excuses or attempt to justify himself. He laid himself bare before God, acknowledging that his sin against Bathsheba was ultimately a sin against God (v. 4). This is important because when we confess our sin, we aren't worried about explaining it away or justifying ourselves. Rather, we are eager to drag our sin into the light of Christ and receive the forgiveness we find at the cross.

We don't confess our sin in order to be forgiven. The cross means our sin has already been forgiven, and the empty tomb and ascension mean we share in Christ's victory by faith. We can confess our sin with confidence that our guilt and shame has already been removed, and we ask the Lord to replace our desire for sin with a stronger desire for holiness.

Confessing sin then covering it up does the opposite of putting the gospel on display. Sometimes Christians feel like confessing their sin will bring shame on the gospel. Instead, that attitude tells the world that we don't really believe God is as merciful and gracious as we say he is.

Obviously, we want to be wise and discerning about whom we confess our sin to and how to do that. But when we confess our sin, we do so with full honesty and confidence that God really does save sinners. The Psalms are an incredible example of what confession and restoration look like in the believer's life.

GOSPEL CLARITY: ICONIC UNITY IN CHRIST

Christians have been "united with Christ" (Philippians 2:1). This is a biblical teaching that, through the indwelling of the Holy Spirit, we have been joined to Christ by faith.

We see this in passages such as Romans 8:1 and 1 Peter 5:14 that talk about how we are "in Christ." That's not mere wordplay; it's an incredible promise that we've received from God. When God the Father loves us, he loves us with the very same love that he gives to Jesus Christ, and when the Holy Spirit promises to be with us, he will be with us as intimately as he is with Jesus Christ.

The gospel's promise of union with Christ leads us to pray differently. We pray with confidence and assurance that God hears us. Christians don't need to earn God's attention. We are already united with Jesus Christ, the second Person of the Trinity, by faith. And so, we bring our requests, praises, laments, and confessions before God with honesty, humility, and hope because we pray as dearly loved sons and daughters.

When these truths are manifested in our relationship with God, we're able to embrace our identity as God's icons in this world. But when we stop praying, our faith can easily become a set of truths about who God is and what he's done in the past rather than a living and vibrant expression of personal intimacy with God.

I hope this chapter reminds you about the personal nature of our identity as image-bearers. God didn't create us as his icons then abandon us. Through the gospel, he has united us to Christ and given us the Holy

Spirit so that we can be joyfully iconic in every circumstance, even during seasons of suffering and lament.

Questions for Reflection

1. What are the different types of psalms mentioned in this chapter?
2. Do you tend to find it easy or difficult to pray? Which type of prayer do you tend to practice?
3. Which of these other types of prayers do you want to learn more about and why?

Chapter 5
Iconic Wisdom

How many of us have made plans for our lives, only for them to blow up in our faces? Maybe a friend betrayed your trust, your potential prom date started seeing someone else, the university you had your heart set on rejected your application, or you didn't get that perfect job. Or maybe you feel like your own decisions have ruined your future dreams, and you're not sure where to go from here. What will you do when your plans get disrupted? And how should you make those plans in the first place?

It's easy to get stressed out and anxious about big decisions, but the small decisions we make every day actually carry far more impact over the course of our lives: how to reply when a friend says something hurtful, what kind of teammate we'll be, whether or not to receive correction from a teacher you don't like, and how you'll treat your family members on a daily basis. The small decisions shape us into the people who make bigger decisions. The Bible might not directly address your particular situation, but it can teach you how to grow in wisdom today. When you're growing in godly wisdom, you'll be better prepared to make those big decisions.

This is where a few of the books classified as "wisdom literature" are really helpful. The book of Job (pronounced *jobe*) addresses suffering, Ecclesiastes talks about living a meaningful life, and Proverbs counsels us to live with wisdom. Lots more could be said about each of these books of the Bible, but if you want to live as an icon of God in every season of life, these books are a gold mine.

One of the most difficult challenges to living as God's icon is what that looks like when life is painful, so let's start there.

JOB: A SUFFERING ICON

Living as icons of God begins by remembering who God is and who we are. This is especially true when life is painful and difficult. Personal suffering can cloud our knowledge of God and make us doubt what we have previously believed with confidence. This is why it's important to prepare for suffering ahead of time by building a foundation for your faith that you can rely on when your feelings and experiences might otherwise lead you astray. God is the holy Creator of all things and we are his image-bearers. He doesn't treat us like slaves or like chess pieces on a board, but as a loving heavenly Father. Yet suffering exists. This is where the book of Job is so helpful, not because it provides a clear-cut answer to the problem of suffering, but because it reminds us how to approach it as faithful icons.

Job suffered. A lot. He's described as a man who was "blameless and upright; he feared God and shunned evil" (Job 1:1). After suffering the loss of all his wealth, all his children, and even his own health, Job asked hard questions about his suffering. Yet "in all this, Job did not sin by charging God with wrongdoing" (1:22). At the end of the book, God shows up and although he rebukes Job for speaking "words without knowledge" (38:2), he assures Job that his suffering wasn't a punishment, but rather a test. Then God restores Job's health, blesses his family, and doubles his wealth.

When we suffer, we have a few options. Some people get angry and blame God, others bargain with God to persuade him to end their suffering, while others entrust themselves to God and seek shelter in his provision. We see those three responses in the book of Job too. Job's wife chose the "curse God and die" option, losing faith in God's character and deciding he's a monster. His friends choose the "what did you do?" option, concluding his suffering must be the result of sin. Thus, they tried to help him figure out what he did wrong so he could repent and hopefully assuage God's judgment. We all know people today who respond to suffering like Job's wife and friends, don't we?

Throughout the book of Job, he insists that he hasn't done anything to deserve this suffering, and he begs God to come and explain himself. Job defends himself, expressing his deep confusion and feelings of betrayal, even while he continues to trust and honor the Lord. When God shows up, he confirms Job's innocence, but he also puts Job in his place by saying things like "Where were you when I laid the earth's foundation? Tell me, if you understand" (38:4), and "Can you raise your voice to the clouds and cover yourself with a flood of water? Do you send the lightning bolts on their way? Do they report to you, 'Here we are'?" (38:34–35).

Afterward, Job realizes God is God and he has every right to do as he pleases. We are out of line when we look at God and tell him that he's running the world wrongly by allowing suffering to exist. Like Job, we need to recognize that we are not God and we don't know what he knows.

Like Job, perhaps you've experienced suffering that doesn't make sense. Or maybe you're looking around at our world and you're struggling to make sense of how a good and sovereign God could allow so much suffering to exist. These are entirely fair questions, and the Bible never rebukes people for asking them. But Jesus himself says, "I have spoken to you of earthly things and you do not believe; how then will you believe if I speak of heavenly things?" (John 3:12). Faith doesn't make our questions or doubts go away. It doesn't sprinkle magic fairy dust around us that will make us happy and comfortable. But it does anchor our security in who God is, and faith guides us to bear his image in a way that reflects confidence in his goodness and power at all times.

I know this doesn't explain why suffering exists, but it is a good place to start. Any biblical answer to the problem of suffering needs to begin with the holiness of God, and that's what the book of Job offers. None of us can judge God, as if he needs to explain himself to us. I know that's hard and can rub people the wrong way, but God's response to Job is entirely proper. God created the heavens and earth. He governs its daily operation and reigns supreme over all things. We are neither his judges nor his advisers, as if our great wisdom would help God do a better job. Besides, who among us knows how much suffering God has prevented from happening in the first place?

When it comes to the big picture of understanding suffering, we need to begin with what we know for sure: God is holy, God is love, God is merciful, and God created people in his image. That means we can trust his judgment. We can trust his almighty rule over creation, even when we are suffering. Sin has corrupted God's good and peaceful creation. As a result, we experience all kinds of hardship and pain, but it will be made right again. Suffering will not have the last word. He is making all things new. Until then, we faithfully endure as God's icons who display the glory and goodness of God in this broken-but-mending world. This is why it's so important for us to learn how to live with iconic wisdom in a variety of situations.

PROVERBS: LIVING WITH WISDOM

Think about the book of Proverbs as a father's wisdom being passed to the next generation. Not every proverb is a hard-and-fast rule that's always true, but they are general truths that will lead you toward wisdom. There are two big themes we need to understand in order to read Proverbs well: the "fear of the LORD," and wisdom versus folly.

The fear of the LORD

One of the central themes of Proverbs is this: "The fear of the LORD is the beginning of wisdom, and knowledge of the Holy One is understanding" (Proverbs 9:10). The phrase *fear of the* LORD shows up ten times throughout the book of Proverbs and is connected to wisdom, the blessing of a long life, godly living, and humility. When there is no fear of God, there is foolishness, arrogance, and reckless living—all of which are contrary to what it means to live as a faithful icon of God.

When Proverbs mentions "the fear of the LORD," it isn't describing fear as a negative emotion that drives us away from God in terror. Instead, it's a positive word that describes our attitude and posture toward God. Sometimes it's helpful to understand what something is by thinking about what it isn't. For example, consider what it would mean to live with no fear of the Lord—to treat God as a harmless genie in the sky or an imaginary myth. Living with the fear of the Lord, however, means we approach God with great humility and reverence because we recognize his holiness and authority.

Of course, the gospel proclaims that this same fearful God is the one we call "our Father in heaven" (Matthew 6:9), but the fear of the Lord is an important reminder about who our Father really is. He is the Creator, Sustainer, and Judge of all things. He is not our bro. Fearing God means we recognize that he is the true judge against whom we have sinned and that he could rightfully smite us any moment he wants to. Thankfully, in his mercy, he has instead clothed us in grace and called us sons and daughters through Christ. Therefore, we approach him with fearful love.

Because we fear God, we approach him with honor, respect, and reverence. Because he is our Father in heaven, we approach him with confidence and joy. These are twin convictions that shape our relationship with God. This shapes more than the way we pray. The fear of the Lord leads us in obedience because we know that God's commandments should not be easily ignored or treated lightly. If God's Word teaches us to do or avoid something, then we should listen! When we lose the fear of God, we begin to view God's commands as little more than advice—some of it good, some of it once good but perhaps now outdated, and some obviously irrelevant for today.

Proverbs teaches us that the fear of the Lord guides us toward humility, godliness, and wisdom because we know that God (and thus, God's Word) is good and true. It also teaches us that one day we will give an account for whether we have lived with wisdom or folly.

Wisdom and folly

There is a difference between knowledge and wisdom. Google can give you knowledge, and education can fill your brain with information. You learn information, but you grow in wisdom. This is true because wisdom doesn't come to those who think they already know everything. So if you want to live with wisdom, it will take time, humility, and a teachable spirit.

Proverbs talks about wisdom and folly as two women who call out to passersby. Lady Wisdom calls out, "Choose my instruction instead of silver, knowledge rather than choice gold, for wisdom is more precious than rubies, and nothing you desire can compare with her" (8:10–11). But Lady Folly lures the simpleminded by promising pleasure and fulfillment through secret and sinful behavior: "Stolen water is sweet; food eaten in secret is delicious!" (Proverbs 9:17).

Proverbs is full of contrasts between wisdom and foolishness in order to help the faithful bear God's image well:

> The way of fools seems right to them,
> but the wise listen to advice. (Proverbs 12:15)

> A fool spurns a parent's discipline,
> but whoever heeds correction shows prudence.
>   (Proverbs 15:5)

> Those who trust in themselves are fools,
> but those who walk in wisdom are kept safe.
>   (Proverbs 28:26)

If wisdom begins with the fear of the Lord, then foolishness begins by looking to yourself as your most reliable guide. Instead of seeking wisdom from God and from others, fools refuse advice, get offended by correction, and always have an excuse for their sin. They believe if it will feel good right now then do it, and if you want it now then go get it. But the wise see through the emptiness and false promises of that lifestyle.

As image-bearers, we all carry a certain amount of wisdom that's embedded into our humanity to guide us, but this doesn't mean we should simply follow our own hearts. Ultimately, wisdom comes from God. This is why wise people don't merely listen to themselves or seek wisdom from within. True wisdom is found through listening to the counsel and insight of others, and it's ultimately found through God. Instead, the Bible talks about fools as those who follow their own hearts and search for wisdom within. These Proverbs show us that the modern maxims such as "live your truth" and "you do you" aren't new. Rather, they are old—and bad—advice that has simply been repackaged for a new generation.

Do you want to grow in wisdom? It begins with the fear or the Lord, molding our minds and hearts so we make decisions according to God's wisdom, not our own. This doesn't involve a mystical experience before every decision. More likely, it simply means we ask two questions: *What does the Bible say about situations like this?* and *What would a wise and godly person do?* These questions will help us live iconic lives that honor God.

ECCLESIASTES: A MEANINGFUL LIFE

What happens when you get everything you've ever wanted? When you dedicate your time and effort to accomplishing something, and then you succeed? What's next? Where do you go from the top of the podium? In many ways, these questions provide the background for Ecclesiastes. King Solomon had everything that the world says can fulfill us (power, wealth, pleasure, etc.) and he still concluded, "Utterly meaningless! Everything is meaningless" (Ecclesiastes 1:2).

The central message of Ecclesiastes is this: If you live for worldly things, then you're never going to be satisfied. Instead, honor and serve the Lord your God from your youth and then you'll be able to live with peace and contentment when you're old. But instead of simply telling you all the ways this is true, Solomon shows you. He takes you by the hand and walks you through his life to put this truth on display because he's speaking from experience. Imagine a grandfather sitting you down and telling you about his life. He is teaching you how to live your life by telling you about his own experiences.

If you want to live a meaningful life, then chasing knowledge won't get you there because "with much wisdom comes much sorrow; the more knowledge, the more grief" (1:18). Hard work and worldly success are ultimately meaningless because "I must leave them to the one who comes after me. And who knows whether that person will be wise or foolish?" (2:18–19). Pursuing wealth is meaningless because "whoever loves money never has enough; whoever loves wealth is never satisfied with their income" (5:10). This same principle applies to chasing pleasure: "Everyone's toil is for their mouth, yet their appetite is never satisfied" (6:7).

All in all, it comes back to what Solomon says in Ecclesiastes 1:14, "I have seen all the things that are done under the sun; all of them are meaningless, a chasing after the wind." Solomon had it all, he tried it all, and he found all the world's promises hollow. Searching for meaning in worldly things is like chasing the wind: No matter how hard you run, you won't be able to catch it.

Ecclesiastes sounds like it could have been written today because it addresses the big question we all ask: "How can my life truly matter?" That's why I read Ecclesiastes every year on my birthday. It might sound depressing, but it helps me remember what matters most in life. At the end of the book, after walking through all the things that are ultimately meaningless, Solomon concludes,

> Remember your Creator
> in the days of your youth. . . .
> Now all has been heard;
> here is the conclusion of the matter:
> Fear God and keep his commandments,
> for this is the duty of all mankind.
> For God will bring every deed into judgment,
> including every hidden thing,
> whether it is good or evil. (Ecclesiastes 12:1,
>   13–14)

Instead of living with the belief that God is trying to ruin all your fun, remember Solomon's warning. You were created for intimate fellowship with God, which is why all the riches in the world cannot satisfy the human soul. The temptation to live for worldly glory isn't new, which is why it's good for us to visit and revisit the wisdom literature in Scripture.

GOSPEL CLARITY: LIVING WITH ICONIC WISDOM

Very few people choose to become foolish. It usually happens one small decision at a time. As we've seen, the biggest difference between wisdom and foolishness is the fear of the Lord. Fools are focused on building monuments to themselves. They want to make their own greatness known instead of embracing their identity as God's icons in this world. The good news for Christians is this: God gives grace to sinners and fools, adopts them through the work of Jesus Christ, and fills them with the Holy Spirit, who makes them wise. If you identify more with fools than with the wise, then welcome to the club! This is a prerequisite for receiving the gospel.

Everyone reading this book is a sinner who needs Jesus. And thankfully, that's exactly who God provides to us!

Be encouraged. You don't need to learn wisdom on your own. In fact, I hope this chapter has made it clear that you actually *cannot* learn wisdom on your own! Ultimately, wisdom comes from God and from God's Word, the Bible. It also comes through fellow Christians who pray for us, encourage us, and even correct us when we're walking in folly. Because of the gospel, we don't need to live in fear of becoming fools. We can walk with confidence that the Holy Spirit is at work in us. When we're living in fellowship with God through Jesus Christ, iconic wisdom guides us in all areas of life so that we reflect his glory and goodness into the world around us.

QUESTIONS FOR REFLECTION

1. Do you find it easier to be iconic when life is comfortable or difficult? Why is that the case?

2. How can the messages of Ecclesiastes and Job help you be iconic when life gets confusing and painful?

3. Describe the differences between someone who fears the Lord and someone who doesn't. How is this related to living with iconic wisdom?

Chapter 6
Iconic Righteousness

One of the most difficult things I needed to do during my teen years was challenge a close friend who was in an unhealthy relationship. We were attending a Christian college, both preparing for pastoral ministry, and he was dating a girl who was dragging him away from Christ. I began to pray for an opportunity to talk about my concern for him, because I knew that speaking up at the wrong time would do no good. Eventually, the right moment came and I said what I felt compelled to say. He didn't necessarily agree with me in the moment, but he understood my intentions and our friendship remained strong. I don't believe that our conversation is what led to their eventual breakup, but I do know that I would've regretted not speaking up, and our friendship was stronger afterward.

The biblical prophets model what it means for us to become advocates of righteousness and godliness when those around us have forsaken the Lord. Most people think prophets spent their time predicting the future and receiving visions from God. Sure, that happened sometimes. But prophets spent most of their time interpreting and applying what God already said to the issues and questions of their day. They were preachers who called Israel to turn away from their sin and to obey God. While there are significant differences between ancient Israel and our modern culture, we are still carrying out the spiritual heritage of the prophets when we call others to believe and obey the Word of God.

In this chapter we're going to study the life and message of Hosea, a prophet whose very life was a living icon of God's steadfast love for Israel, and then we'll walk through a few themes in the prophets that are grounded in the image of God. Finally, I'll address a few cultural hotspots in our own day that the prophets would be likely to address.

HOSEA: AN ICON OF GOD'S STEADFAST LOVE

Hosea lived a strange life. He was a prophet who received a word from the Lord to marry a woman named Gomer. Some of us would love it if God directly told us who he wants us to marry. The problem is that Gomer was a prostitute. She was a sex worker, and he was a prophet of God. An unlikely couple!

Why would God lead a prophet to do this? At that time, the people of Israel were making sacrifices to the Lord so they could claim to keep God's covenant, but they were making sacrifices at other idolatrous temples too. The Lord called Hosea as a prophet to embody God's covenantal love for Israel in order to show Israel the foolishness of their spiritual adultery and the beauty of God's faithful love. Hosea's marriage to Gomer, a woman whom Hosea knew would not be faithful to him, represented God's faithful love and Israel's adultery. Hosea describes his calling this way, "The LORD said to me, 'Go, show your love to your wife again, though she is loved by another man and is an adulteress. Love her as the LORD loves the Israelites'" (3:1). Hosea's life is a literal display of God's message: his faithful love for his faithless people. How iconic!

One of the central messages of Hosea's ministry (and the prophets at large) is "the steadfast love of God." This phrase comes from a Hebrew word, *hesed*. Although there are lots of nerdy books that define *hesed*, my favorite description is found in *The Jesus Storybook Bible*: God's steadfast love is a "never-stopping, never giving up, unbreaking, always and forever love."[1] This is what Hosea's life and ministry uniquely embodied to Israel.

The book of Hosea delivers two messages to us. First, we receive a powerful reminder about the steadfast love of God that stubbornly pursues his children and brings them home to himself. Second, Hosea's example is a faithful model for what it means to be iconic. Although his marriage with Gomer isn't a pattern we should seek to follow in our own lives, the alignment between his life and ministry is powerful. The steadfast love of God is the central message of the prophets, embodied through Hosea and Gomer's marriage. Prophets don't delight in issuing judgment. Rather, they call those who have gone astray to return to God and worship him because he is worthy. But it's not the only message the prophets consistently deliver to Israel.

KEY THEMES IN THE PROPHETS

There are seventeen books in the Bible that are prophetic books. Roughly three hundred years separate Jonah, one of the earliest prophets, and Malachi, the final prophet in the Old Testament. There were other prophets, like Elijah and Elisha, whose ministries were significant and legitimate, but who never wrote books that are included in Scripture. It's important to remember the prophetic books are fairly selective, because many of the prophets lived and preached for decades, so the books couldn't include everything the prophets said and did. That also means it's notable when the prophets are all saying the same thing. Hosea wasn't alone in his concerns for Israel, so below we'll focus on three big themes that are consistent among all the biblical prophets.

Judgment and God's steadfast love

It's common for people who grew up in church to hear about God's love and respond with a shrug. We take God's love for granted, thinking, *Of course God loves us. It's what he's supposed to do.* Israel felt the same way: They were taking God's love for granted. They assumed that because they were children of Abraham, God was obligated to love them.

Listen to the way Isaiah and Jeremiah (who wrote both Jeremiah and Lamentations) talk about God's judgment and steadfast love:

"For the mountains may depart
and the hills be removed,

but my steadfast love shall not depart from
   you,
and my covenant of peace shall not be
   removed,"
says the LORD, who has compassion on you.
   (Isaiah 54:10 ESV)

The steadfast love of the LORD never ceases;
his mercies never come to an end. . . .
Though he cause grief, he will have compassion
according to the abundance of his steadfast
   love.
(Lamentations 3:22, 32 ESV)

God's love doesn't mean he will ignore Israel's sin, and his holiness doesn't mean he delights in judging sinners. Some people assume God's love and holy judgment are in conflict, as if he chooses between one or the other depending on the moment. But that's not what we see in Scripture. God's holiness and love are attributes of who God is. He is perfectly and eternally holy, and he is perfect love. His judgment doesn't flow from anger, but from holiness and steadfast love. This is why God's people can trust his judgment. It's also why the prophets routinely talk about God's judgment and his steadfast love in the same breath.

The prophets were like lawyers, sent by God to warn Israel about the lawsuit coming their way if they continued to sin. God made his commandments to Israel very clear through the covenants, and they chose to repeatedly break covenant with God. His impending judgment should not have been surprising because God had already repeatedly warned his people about the consequences of breaking his commandments. Yet they continued to sin and follow their own desires.

The steadfast love of God doesn't give up on sinners and it doesn't delight in their judgment. In love, God pursued Israel, pleading with them to turn away from their sin and to remember the steadfast love of God. This is also why, even in messages of judgment for their covenant-breaking sin, God also promised an eventual restoration. God's commandments were never a pathway to "earning your salvation." The prophets called Israel to obey God's commandments out of love, not obligation. The love of God is, and always has been, the greatest promise and the richest treasure of God's people.

Idolatry

When you think about idolatry, what comes to mind? Most of us think about a statue that people bow down and make sacrifices to in order to honor or appease the god the idol represents. In certain cultures around the world, this is still a daily reality. But in Western culture, not so much. For us, idolatry takes place exclusively in the heart rather than in a temple.

God is holy. He alone is worthy of our worship and devotion. Although you might not be tempted to worship a statue, you might be drawn to devote yourself to other passions and commitments: friends, hobbies, or things that are really important to you. Sometimes we can find ourselves so devoted to other priorities that we've mostly forgotten God. Sure, you might not literally worship your baseball team or your boyfriend or your GPA, but if you love it and are more committed to protecting it than you are to worshipping Christ Jesus, then it has become an idol in your life. The prophets remind us that if idolatry can creep into Israel after all the miracles they experienced, then surely we should also be on guard. Only then will we be able to help others root out their own idolatries and seek the Lord faithfully (Matthew 7:3–5).

Ancient Israel was alone in their monotheism. They were the only nation that believed the Lord is the Creator of all and that he is the only true God who is worthy of our worship. For a variety of reasons, including a similar desire to conform to the norms of surrounding nations, many Jewish men and women were drawn into idolatry. This is a reminder that long-standing idolatries are difficult to completely leave behind, especially while being surrounded by others who tempt you to simply incorporate worshipping the Lord with other gods. Remember what we already read about Israel's spiritual adultery in Hosea. Nearly every prophetic book addresses this problem. Just look at these examples:

> "Has a nation ever changed its gods?
> (Yet they are not gods at all.)
> But my people have exchanged their glorious
>   God
> for worthless idols." (Jeremiah 2:11)

> "This is what the Sovereign LORD says: Repent! Turn from your idols and renounce all your detestable practices!" (Ezekiel 14:6)

It's easy for us today to wonder what Israel was thinking, because idolatry isn't usually on our minds. But every nation in antiquity practiced idolatry, and we do too. The idolatrous statues of ancient pagan nations were physical symbols (icons) of the nation's deities. Rather than worshipping one Creator God over all nations, they worshipped local gods and spirits whom they thought would protect and provide for the people in that region.

We are called to worship God alone and to reject all other gods. It's frighteningly easy for us to make worldly success and pleasure the most important thing in our lives. Most Christians wouldn't intentionally shift their priorities that way, but it happens on the sly—one decision, one day, one exception at a time.

For example, when there's a schedule conflict between your hobbies and church, does church always get put on the back burner? Of course you can faithfully bear God's image while working hard and enjoying your friends—that's a major emphasis in this book! But if you're always giving God and church your leftover time and attention while giving all your best efforts to other passions, then let that be a warning light about your priorities.

Justice

If God's people want to honor the Lord as faithful icons, it will require more than right theology about what he's like. It must also include treating others in a way that displays God's own heart. This is why justice is at the heart of the prophetic books. Many of the prophets issued harsh judgments against Israel for overlooking injustice and failing to speak up for the oppressed. Listen to God's words to Israel through the prophets Amos and Micah:

"I hate, I despise your religious festivals;
your assemblies are a stench to me.
Even though you bring me burnt offerings and
    grain offerings,
I will not accept them.
Though you bring choice fellowship offerings,
I will have no regard for them.
Away with the noise of your songs!
I will not listen to the music of your harps.
But let justice roll on like a river,
righteousness like a never-failing stream!"
    (Amos 5:21–24)

He has told you, O man, what is good;
and what does the Lord require of you
but to do justice, and to love kindness,
and to walk humbly with your God?
    (Micah 6:8 esv)

God is after more than lip service. He wants true worshippers—image-bearers who will do more than go through the motions of worship. Israel was guilty of developing financial systems that took advantage of the poor, and Amos calls them to repent for it. He even says that God will not receive their worship because their hypocrisy stinks.

Far too many people—both in the prophets' day and in our own—think that justice is optional for God's people. Unfortunately, justice has become a political tactic used to make oneself look righteous while condemning the other political party. As Christians, we need to put such baggage aside and simply recognize the Bible calls each of us to justice and righteous living, because we are iconic of the righteous King who delivers perfect justice.

The reality is, every survivor of injustice is an image-bearer, and the injustice they've endured is a sin against the One they represent. In this way, injustice is always a sin and offense against God himself. Bearing God's image leads us to walk in justice and to oppose injustice, because we know how much we have received through the mercy of God and we are committed to being agents of reconciliation in this world and the next. But what does that look like for us today?

GOSPEL CLARITY: LIVING WITH ICONIC RIGHTEOUSNESS TODAY

The image of God is at the heart of so many issues youth and young adults encounter today, and there's a tendency to either withdraw from hard conversations or to enter them combatively. Some people view themselves as modern-day prophets who will take a hard stand for the truth while viewing compassion as weakness, while others try to make a difference through servanthood while side-stepping direct answers about their views on controversial topics. This has led to lots of confusion among young people about the best way to advocate for God's truth in our culture. That's why this section of "Gospel Clarity" is longer than other chapters.

Below is one example about how the gospel fuels iconic righteousness in the conversation about gender and sexuality, followed by a lengthier reflection about the Christian's posture in a hyper-tolerant age.

Gender and sexuality

As we've already explored in chapter 2, the Bible teaches that gender and sexuality is anchored in what it means to be human, and what it means for men and women to bear God's image. If our gender and sexuality is a visible symbol of the intimacy between Christ and his church, then embracing LGBTQ+ lifestyles cannot reflect that theological truth. Homosexuality breaks down this symbolism by introducing two people who are the same rather than different. Transgender identities turn God's creation of male and female from something the Bible calls "very good" into a socially constructed gender expression that is uniquely determined by each individual person. Compassionate Christianity doesn't compromise on biblical truth.

A prophetic approach to gender and sexuality today begins with God's love for his image-bearers. In love, he has revealed himself through the Bible so we can know who he is and how to be reconciled to him as children of God. Confessing faith in Christ also includes confessing our sin and turning away from it. This is why we're willing to tell others that it's sinful to embrace homosexuality and transgender identities, because not doing so will make it more difficult for them to confess their sin and receive the gracious love of Christ. But if we have those conversations without expressing genuine love, then we are little more than obnoxious cymbals (1 Corinthians 13:1). Like the prophets who called Israel to repentance, we want those who struggle with same-sex attraction or gender dysphoria to be reconciled to God, according to his steadfast love through Jesus Christ. The same way that the prophets warned Israel of their injustices and idolatry, knowing they would likely be ignored, we have an obligation to bear God's image faithfully in our world. Israel's repentance was never the responsibility of the prophet; being a faithful messenger was. It's the same for us too.

Worldly tolerance

The world expresses tolerance as "you do you" and "live your truth." This approach believes everyone's truth is a different version of the overall truth. Hence, in this misguided way of thinking, all religions basically teach the same thing and are equally good, so long as they make you happy and teach you to treat others with kindness.

Tolerance does have its limits, however. If you threaten someone else's safety (physical or emotional), then according to worldly tolerance, you have forfeited the right to be tolerated. When that happens, you've been "canceled." How should Christians respond to this?

Worldly tolerance undermines the very need for tolerance by claiming that conflicts are the result of misunderstandings, not irreconcilable disagreements. *If we really understood one another*, they say, *then we'd realize everyone's viewpoint is equally valid*. But tolerance assumes disagreement. Without a disagreement, where's the need for tolerance at all? Instead of embracing the world's view of tolerance, I think it's wise for Christians to recover a view of tolerance that embraces our differences and disagreements without minimizing them.

Jesus taught his disciples to love their neighbor as themselves (Matthew 22:39) and to love their enemies

(Luke 6:27–28). That's why I define Christian tolerance this way: respect despite disagreement. It's an expression of loving our neighbor and loving our enemy. We should do more than simply put up with those who are different from us. Instead, we should respect them as fellow image-bearers. Disagreement remains, but we disagree with love and respect.

Living with iconic righteousness today will lead you into difficult conversations that require courage, like the conversation with my friend that I shared at the beginning of this chapter. But we need to enter these difficult conversations with wisdom and humility—neither apologizing for the truth or our convictions, nor speaking with a brashness that unlovingly "says it like it is."

This is the prophetic mission: to invite sinners to turn away from their sin and receive the steadfast love of God through Jesus Christ. We must speak God's truth in love to people who need to hear it, recognizing that our message will often be costly. Living as icons of God in this world means we are ambassadors of Christ, pleading with everyone to be reconciled to God and restored as icons who radiate with the glory of God.

QUESTIONS FOR REFLECTION

1. How was Hosea's life an icon of God's steadfast love for Israel? How can this be a helpful example for us?
2. Why is it so tempting for us to call out other people's idolatries without acknowledging our own?
3. How does our natural hatred of injustice flow from the image of God within us?

Chapter 7
Iconic Gospel

Asking teenagers, "What is the gospel?" usually gets me a lot of eye rolls, especially from church kids. They feel like the question is so basic it's beneath them. For many who grew up in the church, the gospel is like gravity—they know what it is but not how to explain it. But the gospel is the message of life that nourishes the Christian, and it's the very heart of what makes us children of God. The gospel is the message of life that we share with others so they can receive the steadfast love of God. That makes it really important for every Christian to know how to articulate the gospel.

Other chapters in this book are seemingly more practical than this one. They will help you discover who you are by helping you discover what you are, as a human being made in God's image. But without this chapter, everything else in this book falls apart. The gospel is good news that God saves sinners. It's an announcement about who Jesus is and what he's done to redeem and restore his image-bearers from sin so they will live in the steadfast love of God for eternity. Without the gospel, trying to live an iconic life is an exercise in self-righteous effort. With that in mind, let's get clear on the gospel.

Jesus Is the Gospel

The gospel is so much more than a good idea. It's not a set of theological statements or philosophical principles that we agree with. The gospel is good news about the person and work of Jesus Christ. It was first announced by the angels who brought the shepherds "good news that will cause great joy for all the people" (Luke 2:10). The good news they declared wasn't a theological statement but a birth announcement. It proclaims Jesus Christ: who he is and what he's done. Simply put, Jesus is the gospel.

After I've spent nearly twenty years in youth ministry, one of my biggest concerns is how few teenagers can articulate the gospel when they graduate from high school. And when I talk about this concern with youth leaders, some of them seem unable to clearly explain the gospel too! When you ask teenagers and youth leaders to answer "What is the gospel?" they tend to give one of three answers:

- A dictionary answer: The gospel means "good news."
- A God-is-love answer: It's a message about God's love for sinners.
- A theological answer: It declares that we can be saved from our sin by believing in Jesus's death and resurrection.

Each of these is true, in a sense. But they're incomplete on their own. Dictionary answers rightly tell us the gospel is good news about what God has done, not good advice for us to accomplish. Meanwhile, God-is-love answers highlight the relational side of the gospel. And theological answers unpack how the gospel saves a person. Each of these answers capture an important aspect of the gospel, but there's more.

I cannot tell you how many times I've been to a youth event where the evangelist failed to preach the gospel. Sure, they preached about the gospel, but they never actually preached the gospel. Here's an example of what this looks like:

> Many of us are stressed and anxious and depressed. Maybe you've tried to deal with it on your own and have realized that you need help. I want to encourage you to trust in Jesus. He is full of love and compassion and will give you the peace of God. Jesus has overcome the world and is victorious over all the things that can make you anxious. So if you want to experience the peace of God, then trust in Jesus by making him your Lord and Savior today. Pray with me if you'd like to receive this kind of peace tonight.

Now, you might be wondering what's wrong with that message. Although it mentions Jesus and talks about a fruit of the gospel (the peace of God), the emphasis is on what the gospel does for you, promises it will be given to you, but never actually invites you to know and love and serve Jesus Christ. I'm not being nitpicky or overly critical here. I've seen far too many students pray for God's help during these types of messages and then wonder why the gospel didn't work. They were promised the fruit of the gospel without actually receiving the gospel.[1] A better invitation would have been to urge students to come to Jesus Christ—"God with us" (Matthew 1:23)—whose victory over sin and death becomes our victory by faith. Our problems will not magically go away, but we will receive the promises of God because we are with Jesus.

The gospel is good news that God saves sinners through Jesus Christ. This brings all three types of answers together and enables us to elaborate in ways that are appropriate for the moment. We rejoice in the gospel because it's an invitation into the steadfast love of God, revealing who Jesus is and what he did. When Christians say "God loves me," it's not a small or cheap thing that rises or falls based on their own feelings. It is perfect, holy, unchanging love that God the Father gives to God the Son, and because we are united with Christ through the Holy Spirit, we also receive that love. That's the kind of love Jesus welcomes us into!

Throughout this book, I've described the iconic life as one that displays God's nature and character to others. Jesus is the literal embodiment of that life, so we will never understand what it means to bear God's image without understanding the person and work of Jesus Christ.

Who Jesus Is: The Person of Christ

Jesus is the main character of the Bible. The Bible is God's way of making himself known to us so we can be restored into perfect fellowship with him. He isn't just an important part of the gospel—he *is* the gospel! Colossians 1:15–16 says this about Jesus: "The Son is the image of the invisible God, the firstborn over all creation. . . . All things have been created through him and for him."

What's the difference between Jesus as the image of God and people as the image of God? Jesus does not merely bear God's image, he is the fullness of God in person. If we are thumbprints, then Jesus is the thumb. If we are mirrors, then he is the face looking into it that we reflect. If we hope to be iconic of God, then Jesus is the one we point to. The Christian life is all about Jesus: We are saved by faith in him and united with him through the indwelling of the Holy Spirit. This is why Christians often talk about sanctification (the journey of growing in Christlikeness) as "becoming more like Jesus" (cf. 2 Corinthians 3:18).

There are a few important biblical truths that help us understand Jesus. He didn't simply show up at the beginning of the New Testament. He is the second person of the Trinity and was actively involved in creation (John 1:1–3). To shake hands with Jesus while he was on earth was to shake the hand of God. To see Jesus was to see God himself (John 14:9–10). This is because, as we've already seen, Jesus is the perfect image of God in human flesh. Hebrews 1:3 even says, "The Son is the radiance of God's glory and the exact representation of his being." Beginning with his miraculous conception, the eternal God the Son has a blood type, a DNA sequence, and distinct fingerprints. If this doesn't bring an awestruck smile to your face, then you've grown far too familiar with the Christmas story!

Every year during Christmastime, we hear John 1:14: "The Word became flesh and made his dwelling among us." But what does this mean? Jesus is one person with two natures: a human nature and a divine nature. It's important to recognize that natures don't act—people do. His natures coexisted with perfect harmony within his person, so his person was 100 percent divine nature and 100 percent human nature.

Jesus's humanity and divinity don't combine to make a combined nature, like lemonade and iced tea combining to make an Arnold Palmer. They don't take turns being "active" depending on the moment, as if his humanity is working while he eats and sleeps and his divinity is working when he teaches and performs miracles. He isn't a demigod like fictional characters such as Hercules or Percy Jackson, whose human natures were supercharged by their divinity. And his humanity isn't overpowered by his divinity like a cricket chirping at a rock concert. Jesus really is fully human—in every way like us, except without a sinful nature.

Our non-Christian friends consider Jesus nothing more than another human teacher. In response, it's tempting for Christians to talk about his identity as the Son of God so much that we hardly talk about his humanity at all. That's a mistake. The verses above clearly teach that Jesus is God. At the same time, Jesus was a real human. He needed to learn and grow and mature. Luke 2:52 even says, "And Jesus grew in wisdom and stature, and in favor with God and man." Just imagine being Jesus's teacher or beating him in a footrace when you were growing up together!

Jesus was aware of his true identity (Luke 2:42–49), but he had a normal childhood. We can sometimes think Jesus had an unfair advantage and he was able to know everything and perform miracles because he had superhuman powers. Instead, we consistently see him trusting in the Father to heal and provide and give wisdom.

The image of God is what we are and directs how we live. Similarly, Jesus shows us what it looks like to be the fullness of the image of God. We've seen this through who Jesus is. Now let's see what he did.

WHAT JESUS DID: THE WORK OF CHRIST

Jesus is fully God and fully human, but what did he accomplish? It doesn't take much time to look around and see a lot of brokenness and sin in the world. Honestly, it doesn't take much time to look around and see a lot of brokenness and sin in the church either!

Think of it this way: If Jesus came only to judge all creation, then the only people with any hope of salvation would have been faithful Jewish men and women who had received and obeyed the entire Old Testament law. And if Jesus came to remove all the sin from the earth without giving us new hearts, then it would've been like a repeat of Noah and the flood. Virtually all the sinners would be removed, but because even the godly people were sinners, things would regress again within a generation or two.

This is why God's salvation unfolds as we read the New Testament. God's plan extends to all image-bearers, not only to Israel, and that takes time. Jesus came to fulfill the Old Testament prophecies about a coming Savior. He made it possible for us to receive new hearts that empower us to be conformed to the image of Christ. And he will return again to finish everything he started.

It's important for us to remember what Jesus did as we wait for his return, when he'll finish what he started (more on this in chapter 9). When Christians think about the gospel, many tend to only think about the cross and empty tomb. There's a good reason for that, but there are four important aspects of Jesus's work that are good news for us to celebrate.

Jesus's perfect righteousness

Jesus lived a holy and sinless life. The whole biblical message of justification—sinners being made right with God—is that we're declared righteous by faith in Jesus Christ because his perfect righteousness is applied to us. If we believe that, then we should take some time to understand it. In Romans 5:12–21 and 1 Corinthians 15:20–49, the apostle Paul presents Jesus as what theologians refer to as the "second Adam" because Jesus succeeds where Adam failed. Both were born without sin, and both bore God's image. But where Adam gave into temptation, Jesus remained faithful. It might help to compare Adam's temptation with Jesus's temptation.

We read about Jesus's temptations in Luke 4:1–13. The first temptation of Christ brings him face-to-face with his own hunger, and the devil tempts him to provide for himself. Where Adam gave into the temptation to eat what was forbidden, Jesus doesn't. Then, just like the devil offered Adam knowledge and power that only belong to God, Jesus is offered a theoretical shortcut to becoming Lord over all nations. Still, Jesus refuses, saying, "It is written: 'Worship the Lord your God and serve him only'" (Luke 4:8). Finally, the devil tells Jesus to jump off the temple so the angels would rescue him in an impressive display of glory. It's easy to hear echoes in this of the serpent's promise to Adam: "You will not certainly die" (Genesis 3:4). Jesus overcomes temptation by trusting the Word of God and resisting the false promises of the tempter. Jesus is the second Adam, perfect in righteousness, faithful through temptation.

Theologians refer to Jesus's perfect righteousness as "active obedience": He obeyed God's law perfectly and without any sin. Again, it's important to remember what we've said above regarding his humanity: He didn't simply get a free pass excusing him from temptation because he is fully God and fully human. Hebrews 4:15 says Jesus's ministry to us is so powerful precisely because he "has been tempted in every way, just as we are—yet he did not sin." He resisted temptation because he trusted his Father in heaven and saw through the lies and false promises of the tempter.

As you and I strive to grow in godliness and live as faithful icons of God, Jesus's perfect righteousness does more than forgive our sins; it strengthens us when we face temptation.

Jesus's sinless death and substitutionary atonement

Jesus didn't suffer and die on the cross out of obligation. And he didn't do it because we are worthy. God didn't look at people and think, *Wow, they're just so wonderful. I really don't feel complete without them*. The Bible says that we became "God's enemies" because of our sin (Romans 5:10; cf. Colossians 1:21). But in his steadfast love, God sent Jesus as the rescue for our sin even though we deserved his wrath (Ephesians 2:1–5).

Have you ever wondered how Jesus's death on the cross could save us? The Bible lays the foundation for the cross through the sacrificial system in the Old Testament, where people would bring a flawless lamb before the priest as a sacrifice. This is why John the Baptist called Jesus "the lamb of God, who takes away the sin of the world" (John 1:29).

Through the cross, the person and work of Jesus Christ came together to fulfill the symbolism of the Old Testament sacrificial system. All those sacrificial lambs pointed Israel toward the perfect Lamb of God who would take away the sin of the world through his own sacrifice. The judgment and wrath our sin rightfully deserves were poured out on Jesus. And he satisfied it fully.

Jesus's victorious resurrection

The resurrection of Jesus shows that he didn't merely take our sin's judgment, he conquered sin itself. Sin and death always go hand in hand throughout Scripture. Whenever you see one, the other is always present. This was true in the garden of Eden, it's true throughout the Bible, it's true in our own experience, and it will be true in the new heavens and new earth.

Sometimes this connection between sin and death is really obvious in our lives, and other times it's lurking in the shadows through the death of a friendship or the obvious injustice of someone getting away without consequences for their sin. Jesus's resurrection from the grave showed his victory over sin and death. Their grip on humanity and creation has been broken!

This is why baptism is such a powerful and enduring sign of salvation. Whether you believe in believer's baptism or infant baptism, it is a visible expression of the gospel. Romans 6:1–14 presents a beautiful and powerful explanation of why the resurrection of Christ means that Christians must not continue to live in sin. It's worth taking a moment to read that whole passage, but here's a sample: "The death he died, he died to sin once for all; but the life he lives, he lives to God. In the same way, count yourselves dead to sin but alive to God in Christ Jesus" (vv. 10–11).

Christ Jesus's victory over sin and death is the reason we can live with confidence and hope. He has already overcome sin and death, so what else is there to fear?

Jesus's ascension into glory

Have you ever thought about what Jesus is doing today? For the longest time, I believed that Jesus ascended into glory (Acts 1:6–11) without giving it any meaningful thought or consideration. Honestly, I thought about it as if Jesus is hibernating: He came, died, rose from the grave, and then went up to heaven to take a nice, long nap until it's time to wake up and get back to work. But that's not at all what the Bible says.

The ascension means that Jesus continues to lead and care for his people, except now he's doing so from the right hand of the throne of God rather than from earth (1 Peter 3:22). He is watching over his church, caring for us, and praying for us until it's time for him to return.

Much more can be said about the ascension, but one thing's for certain: Jesus isn't hibernating. He is actively leading his church from heaven. He is watching over you and me, today and every day until he returns. Not only that, but Hebrews 7:25 says that Jesus is praying for you and me! This is part of Jesus's work that we rarely talk about, but it is such a treasure to remember when we feel alone or afraid. Jesus is with us, reigning in glory, and watching over us as he conforms us into his own image.

The gospel includes more than what happened on the cross and empty tomb. Jesus's nature, sinless life, ascension, and return (which will be addressed in chapter 8) shouldn't be overlooked. Without understanding who he is and all that he did, our understanding of the gospel will be limited. Let's celebrate the hope we have because of who Jesus is and all that he's done.

GOSPEL CLARITY: RECEIVING THE ICONIC GOSPEL

Living an iconic life means you desire to bear God's image so others would see the glory and goodness of God through you. To some degree, every human shines God's glory into our world simply because every person is created in God's image, and no amount of sin can take that away. But we cannot reflect God's holiness or goodness apart from the transforming work of the Holy Spirit. We need Jesus. In him, we behold what God is like. He is the perfect image, the One we were created to represent in the first place! And his life shows us what a holy life looks like. Apart from him, our sinful desires and actions would lead us to be self-iconic rather than icons of our heavenly Father.

The gospel of Jesus Christ sets us free. Jesus doesn't come to us with a whip that tells us to try harder, do more, or prove ourselves. He doesn't rank anyone's value based on their level of godliness and doesn't eliminate anyone because their sin is too deep. When we confess our sin and profess faith in Jesus Christ (in who he is and what he's done), we are adopted as children of God according to his steadfast love. We also receive the Holy Spirit, who unites us with Christ (John 14:15–17) and makes us more and more like Jesus (Romans 8:29). He is so faithful to save and restore us. God has not given up on his image-bearers. He never will.

QUESTIONS FOR REFLECTION

1. What is the gospel? How would you explain it to someone who asks?
2. Do you tend to think about Jesus as mostly God and partially human, or vice versa? Why does this matter?
3. How does the ascension of Christ encourage you to remember the gospel in the present tense? Why is this so important?

Chapter 8
Iconic Imitation

Logan is a new Christian but none of his friends are. They already mocked him for attending youth group. What would they say now that he has confessed faith in Jesus Christ? And how should he respond? Logan wants to grow in his new identity in Christ and he wants to honor God, but he's not sure what that means for his friendships. Should he distance himself from them because of their negative influence or hit them hard with their need for Jesus too? What counsel would you offer him?

New Christians often face many of these kinds of questions. There isn't one universally true answer for these situations. But the Bible does give us wisdom to navigate these situations as we learn how to live according to our new identity in Christ.

No one becomes holy by simply being told, "Hey, be holier!" Much of this book has focused on setting a biblical foundation for what it means to be iconic of God's glory and goodness in your world. Now that we've seen how the gospel gives us a new heart that conforms us to the image of Christ, let's focus on what that looks like.

YOU ARE A NEW CREATION

No one becomes a Christian because they want their life to stay the same. If you don't want to change, then you don't actually want Jesus. You probably just want a free ticket to heaven after you die, and that's not Christianity. True, saving faith in Jesus involves two types of confession: confession of sin (admitting the truth about your need for God) and confession of Jesus Christ as Lord (admitting the truth about who God is and what he's done to adopt you as his son or daughter by faith). These confessions acknowledge that we are sinners who need the grace and power of God to save us, change us, and make us holy.

Sometimes new Christians experience radical transformation and freedom from addictions or long-standing temptations. But most of the time, there is a simple and steady change that leads us to grow in godliness over the long haul.

The Bible describes the Christian's new life in a few different ways that reflect the iconic life:

Therefore, if anyone is in Christ, *the new creation* has come: The old has gone, the new is here! (2 Corinthians 5:17, emphasis added)

Do not lie to each other, since you have taken off your old self with its practices and have put on the new self, which is being *renewed in*

knowledge in the image of its Creator. (Colossians
3:9–10, emphasis added)

When the Bible says you are a new creation, it doesn't
mean your life before Jesus is erased and irrelevant. It's
not that you are literally new in every area, but that you
have a new nature. Your sin has been forgiven, and the
Holy Spirit has moved in. You've received a new heart, a
new identity, and new desires. This journey of becoming
holy is called sanctification. That's a fancy word that's
based on the Greek word meaning "to make holy." I like
to describe it as God "holy-izing" people. God saves sinners, declares them holy, and then he makes them so.

Where indwelling sin has corrupted our desire and
ability to reflect God's glory and goodness in the world,
the gospel sanctifies and empowers us to be renewed in
God's image. Where we used to indulge in sin because
we thought it was the best way to enjoy life, now we find
pleasure in obeying God's commandments and in serving others. And while we used to think that being praised
for our accomplishments was the greatest reward for a
job well done, now we want our lives to lift people's eyes
to behold the glory and power of God. In short, sanctification makes us faithful icons of Christ Jesus.

THE ATTRIBUTES OF GOD AND THE FRUIT OF THE SPIRIT

What should the life of a healthy and maturing Christian
look like? The apostle Paul addressed that question by
describing what he calls "the fruit of the Spirit." This
is what the Holy Spirit produces in Christians as they
grow in godliness. Interestingly, the Greek word translated into English as *fruit* is singular. That means that

together, these are the result of God's work in the Christian. Here's what Paul writes:

> But the fruit of the Spirit is love, joy, peace, forbearance, kindness, goodness, faithfulness, gentleness and self-control. Against such things there is no law. Those who belong to Christ Jesus have crucified the flesh with its passions and desires. Since we live by the Spirit, let us keep in step with the Spirit. (Galatians 5:22–25)

Where did Paul get this list? Did he just choose random traits that would be good for Christians to pursue? Godliness and the fruit of the Spirit are anchored in what it means for us to be image-bearers. They are grounded in the nature of God, which is the very heart of what it means for us to bear God's image.

This is an important aspect of bearing God's image that we briefly touched upon in chapter 1. An attribute of God is something that is always true about God. For example, wrath isn't an attribute of God (even though it is accurate to say "God is wrathful") because God wasn't wrathful before sin entered into creation, he won't be wrathful after his final judgment when sin has been judged, nor is he wrathful toward those who have been forgiven through faith in Jesus Christ. God's wrath is best understood as his holy response to sin rather than as an attribute of his unchanging nature.

The "communicable attributes" of God are attributes that God and people have in common. Hence, they "communicate" between God and people. Whereas we bear these attributes in imperfect and incomplete ways, they are perfect and holy in God. These include love and holiness and wisdom, among other things. There are also "incommunicable attributes" that describe characteristics that are unique to God, such as his omnipresence, omniscience, and self-existence.

As we explore the question "What does a maturing Christian look like?," it's helpful to dig into each fruit of the Spirit by recognizing the ways they are anchored in the communicable attributes of God.[1] This will enable us to see how the fruit of the Spirit describes what it means for us to be new creations who are conformed to the image of Christ.

Love

Love is listed first among the fruit of the Spirit. That seems notable. Love is at the heart of who God is, and it's at the heart of who we're becoming as new creations in Christ. The love of God is what motivated him to create anything at all and to redeem sinners, and the love of God should be an undeniable attribute of every Christian. It's so central to the Christian calling that 1 John 4:8 says, "Whoever does not love does not know God, because God is love."

Walking in the love of God is costly—not because we're paying a lot to earn it, but because the love that God extends to sinners is a self-sacrificial love. So if we want to walk in the love of God, then we need to love sinners too!

When was the last time you made a sacrifice (without bitterness) in order to show love to someone? Maybe this involved forgiving someone who offended you or giving away something to meet someone else's need.

When you love God and love others (both your neighbors and enemies), you're really beginning to live an iconic life. People will see your love and good deeds, and they'll give praise to your Father in heaven (Matthew 5:16). This is exactly what it means to be a faithful icon of Jesus Christ.

Joy

God is joyful. He isn't sad or glum. He isn't twiddling his thumbs in boredom on a cloud in heaven. God is eternally and perfectly joyful. I believe this points to one of God's chief attributes: holiness. The word *holy* literally means "set apart." The holiness of God means that he is distinct and different from his creation.

Joy and fear are the result when God's people encounter the holiness of the One they call "our Father in heaven." When God doesn't smite them, their fear turns to joy. For example, consider Psalm 5. It begins, "Listen to my words, Lord, consider my lament. Hear my cry for help, my King and my God, for to you I pray" (vv. 1–2). This is a prayer for protection and deliverance when the psalmist is afraid and in danger.

He continues, "But I, by your great love, can come into your house; in reverence I bow down toward your holy temple. . . . Let all who take refuge in you be glad; let them ever sing for joy" (vv. 7, 11). This song of joy isn't the result of physical security. The psalmist is likely still in the same danger that prompted the prayer. But he sings for joy because he remembers the holiness of the God who hears his prayer.

How do you respond when things don't go your way? Do you get angry or bitter? Do you view yourself as a victim with terrible luck? Or do you keep a positive attitude because you know that your heavenly Father cares for you, even when life goes sideways? This doesn't mean we never get sad or frustrated. But it does mean the Holy Spirit produces the fruit of joy in us, even when life is hard, because we rejoice in the holiness and mercy of our heavenly Father.

Peace

God is not anxious. He doesn't hurry and he isn't stressed. God is perfectly at peace. This is so true that he's built it into the framework of creation. He created everything in six days, but creation wasn't complete until he made the Sabbath on the seventh day. To reinforce this, he even created our bodies to require sleep for a third of our lives! We literally cannot function without rest.

One detail of the Bible's creation story that has always intrigued me is that each daily account of God's creative work in Genesis 1 ends with a summary similar to the following: "And there was evening, and there was morning—the first day" (v. 5). This is repeated for every day except the Sabbath. God's sabbath continues throughout eternity. He reigns over everything he created. And he invites us to share in that rest and reign (Hebrews 4:9–10). This is why Jesus says, "Come to me, all you who are weary and burdened, and I will give you rest" (Matthew 11:28). When we receive the gospel of Jesus Christ, we are invited to lay down our burdens and to follow Jesus in the way of peace. We are invited into God's sabbath.

Do you experience peace or does your stress level rise and fall depending on your emotions? I know so many young men and women who experience very little peace—they are burdened by anxiety and depression. They struggle within their minds and hearts, and many of them wonder if it's the result of weak faith. They wonder if their anxieties and depression would go away if their faith were stronger. If you've felt this way, then I want to assure you that your sabbath is secure in Christ, even if you don't experience it today. Walking in faith sometimes means we cling to God's promises despite what we see and feel. Jesus is faithful. He carries your burdens and invites you to trust that his yoke is easy and his burden is light.

Forbearance

Forbearance isn't a word we use often anymore, but it's closely related to the idea of having a long fuse with people who are rebellious or troublesome. Some translations use the word *patience* to describe this fruit of the Spirit, but the original meaning is stronger and richer than mere patience. This isn't the type of patience we have while waiting for our DoorDash order to arrive. It's the type of patience that's required when your sibling is intentionally pushing your buttons or your bully is provoking you.

This is the kind of forbearance God has toward sinners. Imagine how short-lived our salvation would be if God did not have this attribute. If our standing with God depended on our ability to fulfill God's commandments at all times, then none of us would be able to live with security or confidence. But God forbears with us. As Exodus 34:6 says, "The LORD, the LORD, the compassionate and gracious God, slow to anger, abounding in love and faithfulness."

How do you treat those who are difficult to love? This is the type of love Jesus calls us to when he says, "I tell you, love your enemies and pray for those who persecute you" (Matthew 5:44). This is a shared attribute between God and people as his image-bearers. After all, if we only love those who love us, then how is Christian love any different from worldly love? As we become icons of Christ Jesus, the Holy Spirit leads us to forebear with others as God does with us. This kind of patience makes little sense to non-Christians, especially in today's cancel culture, but it's a powerful demonstration of God's nature and salvation to others.

Kindness

The Greek word that's translated as *kindness* has multiple meanings that cannot be easily captured by one English word. It has to do with active goodness that is useful and practical. That's what makes *kindness* a good translation because it has to do with an act of servanthood that bestows goodness and blessing on the person who receives it. God's kindness is seen in the way he provides and cares for his creation. He is personally invested in his creation, especially his image-bearers. God is not reluctant toward us, and we don't need to approach him as if we need to persuade him to hear our prayers (Matthew 7:11).

Do you seek opportunities to do good to others, or are you so focused on yourself you don't notice the needs of others? Practicing kindness leads us to serve others regardless of their ability to return the favor. When we are living icons of Christ, we are walking in kindness toward others—not with forced or reluctant obligation, but with a generous spirit guided by steadfast love.

Goodness

The spiritual fruit of goodness reflects our calling to live in a way that displays God's glory and goodness. This is about consistently blessing other people. The Bible often talks about God's goodness to all that he has made (e.g., Psalm 145:9). Jesus tells his disciples their goodness will cause others to praise their Father in heaven (Matthew 5:16). Although our good deeds don't contribute to our salvation, they are evidence that we've received new hearts that delight in serving God by serving others.

Are you living so that others would see your goodness and think well of you, or do you want them to see Christ through you? It might be tempting to do good works to improve your honor society application, have a stronger college application, or earn community service awards. But it's better to serve with the simple goal of caring for the people we're serving so that God would ultimately receive the glory. Is it wrong to list those things in your applications? No, it's not. But it's all about your motivation: Why are you doing these good works? When the gospel sets you free from the need to impress others, you'll able to serve with joy, whether you get recognition for it or not. This type of selflessness beautifully displays the glory and goodness of God.

Faithfulness

Sometimes our feelings and experiences can lead us to doubt God's faithfulness. But as we've already seen, God's steadfast love never fails. None of his promises fail (Joshua 21:45; 1 Kings 8:56). God doesn't promise something and then simply change his mind or give up. His steadfast love is the foundation for his children to confidently walk by faith because we know that he will never abandon or give up on his beloved sons and daughters. So if we are suffering, we can suffer with hope and faith because we know our God is rich in steadfast love toward us.

Do you make decisions as if everything is up to you, or do you trust God's faithfulness in your life? This is where faith becomes more than just a good idea. Faith is active trust that God is who he says he is and he will do what he promises—a trust that causes us to live with God in mind.

Unfortunately, it's far too easy to simply make faith a good idea—a set of philosophical truths we believe, but ones that don't factor into real life. Living an iconic life means there will be times when your feelings and eyeballs will tell you that walking by faith makes no sense at all. In those moments, it's good to remember that Jesus says even faith the size of a mustard seed is enough (Matthew 17:20–21). (Google it . . . mustard seeds are very small.) That's because what matters is not how perfect our faith is but the character of the One who is rich in steadfast love. Therefore, we will live by faith because our confidence is in God.

Gentleness

God's gentleness is obvious through the other attributes we've already discussed. This mean that even when God judges and disciplines he does so gently, with proper justice and goodness. We can see this reflected in the prophet Jeremiah's prayer, "Discipline me, Lord, but only in due measure—not in your anger, or you will reduce me to nothing" (Jeremiah 10:24). God is not harsh or wicked, even in judgment.

Are you more likely to be so gentle that you avoid conflict, or do you take a stand for Christ in a way that can be harsh or abrasive? Gentleness is not weakness. It is humility and compassion in action, especially toward those who are vulnerable or weak or toward those who openly mock God. The heart of Christianity is the grace of God, poured out for sinners through Jesus Christ. This is why Christians are told to give the reason for our Christian hope "with gentleness and respect" (1 Peter 3:15). Treating others with gentleness doesn't mean you should become pushover. But it does mean that even in hard situations that require courage, you should embody the gentleness of Christ.

Self-control

Is God self-controlled? It's an interesting question, because how can the One who controls all things be controlled by anything or anyone? The Bible says God always does what is right (Hebrews 6:10), and at the same time, God is free to do whatever he wants (Psalm 135:6). One of God's attributes is his independence. That means that he doesn't rely on anyone or anything else. God is self-controlled in the sense that he always acts according to his own perfect nature. He never does anything that is contrary to his holy nature or attributes.

Do you give in to every desire or want that arises, or do you know how to say no to yourself? Self-control isn't a "no pain, no gain" approach to Christianity. Living without self-control leads Christians to live a life of sinful indulgence, followed by regret and guilt that prompts repentance. And then the cycle repeats the next time they indulge their sinful desires. Sin and temptation twist and pervert God's image within us, and they turn us into someone we weren't created to be. That's why we deny worldly temptations and desires, even if they come so much more naturally than our godly desires. We do this because we want to bear God's image well, and these worldly desires deceive us the same way they deceived Adam and Eve. Self-control empowers us to resist temptation, trust the goodness of God, and to live as his faithful icons in this world.

GOSPEL CLARITY: ICONIC IMITATIONS OF CHRIST

I know this chapter has been long and occasionally heavy. But I think it might be the most important one in the book. Because if you and I are going to imitate Christ and be conformed into his image, then it's important to know what that looks like. When we embody and practice these characteristics, we are sharing in God's communicable attributes. This is an important aspect of what it means for us to be created in God's image. That also means that some unbelievers will have glimmers of these attributes, because they also bear God's image. The fruit of the Spirit isn't a spiritual to-do list—it's a description of what God is doing in us when he conforms us into the image of Christ.

As you grow in your relationship with Jesus, the fruit of the Spirit will help you see the ways God is changing you. Your faith in Jesus has made you new. God has given you a new identity in Christ, he is renewing your heart so you desire the things that please him, and he is molding you into his image. Your Christian maturity won't follow a steady timeline. There will be seasons of growth and seasons of spiritual drought. But God will finish the good work that he has begun in you. How exciting for you and me to become more of what we were created to be!

QUESTIONS FOR REFLECTION

1. What's the difference between the "incommunicable" and "communicable" attributes of God? Which ones highlight what it means for us to be created in God's image?
2. Choose one fruit of the Spirit and explain how it's anchored in one of God's attributes.
3. Put into your own words how the fruit of the Spirit can help you live an iconic life.

Chapter 9
Iconic for Eternity

"**W**hat are you most looking forward to about heaven?" That was my senior pastor's question during staff meeting as he prepared for an upcoming sermon. Other people said something normal such as, "Being in the presence of Jesus," or "Seeing my mother again." Those types of answers got lots of head nods and *mmm's*. But everyone laughed at my answer: "Playing fetch with a cheetah." Everyone laughed because they didn't think I was serious. But I was. I still think that'll be awesome and I can't wait for it to happen!

Yes, I love cheetahs and think it'll be a lot of fun. And of course, I yearn for the day when I'll be with Jesus face-to-face and see loved ones who have died. But to me, playing fetch with a cheetah represents the big picture of living in the new heavens and new earth. The prophet Isaiah uses similar imagery in Isaiah 11:6: "The wolf will live with the lamb, the leopard will lie down with the goat, the calf and the lion and the yearling together; and a little child will lead them." This is so far from today's reality, but it's a beautiful word picture of the ways creation will be restored and glorified. Everything that has been lost and broken in this life will be gloriously perfect in eternity, and I cannot wait for it!

We will bear God's image in God's presence. We will be "transformed into his image with ever-increasing glory" (2 Corinthians 3:18). We'll be perfect and holy in every aspect of bearing the communicable attributes and fruit of the Spirit. But aside from our holiness, what will it look like for us to be transformed in glory? We obviously cannot know everything about what lies ahead, but the Bible does give us enough of a glimpse to live with great hope and anticipation.

Here are four truths about our hope in glory that will help you bear God's image faithfully and courageously today.

THE INTERMEDIARY STATE AND THE NEW HEAVENS AND NEW EARTH

> And I saw what looked like a sea of glass glowing with fire and, standing beside the sea, those who had been victorious over the beast and its image and over the number of its name. (Revelation 15:2)

> Then I saw "a new heaven and a new earth," for the first heaven and the first earth had passed away, and there was no longer any sea. I saw the Holy City, the new Jerusalem, coming down out of heaven from God, prepared as a bride beautifully dressed for her husband. And I heard a

loud voice from the throne saying, "Look! God's dwelling place is now among the people, and he will dwell with them. They will be his people, and God himself will be with them and be their God. 'He will wipe every tear from their eyes. There will be no more death' or mourning or crying or pain, for the old order of things has passed away." (Revelation 21:1–4)

When you think about heaven, what comes to mind? If you're like most people who grow up in a Western church, then you probably think about our spirits worshipping in the presence of Jesus. Eternity is so much more than a long church service in the clouds. This visualization of heaven is shaped more by our children's cartoons than it is by Scripture. This is more representative of what Christian theologians call the "intermediary state" than it is about our eternal destiny in the new heavens and new earth. The intermediary state is the spirit's presence with God after one's death but before the resurrection of the dead.

The Bible talks about the new heavens and new earth as the place where the people of God will spend eternity in the presence of God. No one lives in the new heavens and new earth yet because they won't exist until after Jesus returns and issues his final judgment. Because of this, we need to ask ourselves what Jesus meant by telling the thief on the cross, "Truly I tell you, today you will be with me in paradise" (Luke 23:43).

The new heavens and new earth will be a physical and glorified re-creation without any lingering stain of sin or the curse. This will be established after the final judgment described in Revelation 20. Various scriptures mention a state of existence that brings our souls immediately upon death into the presence of God even though they aren't united yet with resurrection bodies (2 Corinthians 5:6–8; Philippians 1:23). The intermediary state is temporary—it is where our believing loved ones who have already died enjoy the presence of God while they wait for their resurrected bodies. This is what we mean by saying that Christians who die are welcomed immediately into the presence of God. But this is not our eternal status, since we will receive glorified bodies in the new heavens and new earth. Although God is timeless, it doesn't seem as if the intermediary state exists outside of time because the people there have some awareness of what's happening on earth (Revelation 6:9–11). If you'd like more details, join the club. We aren't given many in Scripture. But we are told enough to face death with confidence that we will be with our Savior, there will be great rejoicing with the angels, and we will receive glorified bodies in the new heavens and new earth when Jesus returns to fulfill his victory over sin and death.

Although some people say things like "This world is not my home; I'm just passing through," it's not entirely accurate. To be fair, most people who say this are simply trying to lift our eyes toward our future hope. But it can easily lead us to forget this world actually is our eternal home. God will create a new earth, not a new planet for us to live in. Even if we consider it Eden 2.0, the new heavens and new earth will bear a striking resemblance to Eden. There will be soil, trees, animals, vegetation— and people! In Genesis 1, God called his creation good and said the creation of his image-bearers was very good.

We should live in this earth as preparation for the work and worship we will carry out for all eternity. We will bear God's image in his presence forever in the new heavens and new earth, reflecting his glory and goodness in our glorified bodies.

OUR GLORIFIED BODIES

> So will it be with the resurrection of the dead. The body that is sown is perishable, it is raised imperishable; it is sown in dishonor, it is raised in glory; it is sown in weakness, it is raised in power; it is sown a natural body, it is raised a spiritual body. . . . And just as we have borne the image of the earthly man, so shall we bear the image of the heavenly man. (1 Corinthians 15:42–44, 49)

Did you know that you'll have a physical body in the new heavens and new earth? Creation will be gloriously restored, and if the first creation was full of life, food, play, and rest before sin entered into the picture, then why would they be absent in the new heavens and new earth? We will enjoy every aspect of God's creation to the fullest extent, without any corruption whatsoever.

The longest description of our glorified bodies is found in 1 Corinthians 15:35–58. Paul uses seeds and farming as metaphors to explain spiritual truths of our resurrection bodies (see the passage above). He argues that our physical bodies will be glorified. These glorified bodies will perfectly bear the image of Christ for all eternity, fulfilling our created purpose in the new creation.

Jesus's resurrected body is the template for ours (v. 49). He was a real person and was perfect in holiness and glory. Our resurrected bodies will be like his: human and holy.

Every trace of the curse will be removed from our body. We will no longer experience anything that's the result of God's curse on sin: sickness, disability, disease, pain, suffering, or death. Our bodies will be the pinnacle of human flourishing. Jesus healed many with sickness and disabilities as evidence of the breaking in of the kingdom of God (Luke 7:22). In the fullness of God's glorified creation, fellow image-bearers who were born with various disabilities will live with freedom from disability.[1] We will experience the fullness of life, health, and joy together, bearing God's image to one another and leading each other to worship and adore the Lord.

Our resurrected bodies will be like Christ's resurrected body. Have you ever wondered how Jesus went unrecognized by some of his disciples after the resurrection? When Mary first saw him on Resurrection Sunday, she thought he was a gardener (John 20:15). Later that day, Jesus walked for a long time with two disciples on the Emmaus Road before he opened their eyes to recognize him (Luke 24:13–35). That evening, Jesus appeared to the apostles. They were astounded and Thomas needed to see his nail-pierced hands to believe it was truly him (John 20:19–29).[2]

I don't think these are instances where Jesus used his divine power to make himself unrecognizable. Instead, it seems like there was something truly different about his resurrected body. Jesus's resurrected body foreshadows what our resurrection bodies will be like.

When I was a child, I used to imagine that I had suddenly become omniscient when I was in heaven. It wasn't that I would actually know everything, but that I would think a question and somehow the answer would just come to me, almost like Neo downloading knowledge and skills in the Matrix movies.

As cool as that might be, it's simply not true. In glory, we will be fully and perfectly human. That includes our human limitations. We won't learn how to fly or become telepathic or be able to levitate objects. We will continue to bear God's communicable attributes with glory, but that doesn't mean we'll begin to express God's incommunicable attributes (omniscience, omnipresence, sovereignty, etc.). We will still be human image-bearers—remember, we'll be holy and human. All this leads me to believe (although Scripture doesn't explicitly say so) that we'll eat, sleep, and have "bodily functions" with perfect health.

We will have physical bodies, and the book of Revelation even talks about "the nations" (21:24) being present in the new creation and different languages being spoken (7:9) there, which indicates that our ethnicity and cultures will remain. We won't suddenly become one homogenous group of men and women who speak a heavenly language. Koreans will still be Koreans, the French will still be French, and the Irish will still be Irish. We will bear God's image together, displaying that no culture can do that fully; rather, it requires a diversity of cultures to display his honor and glory like a holy kaleidoscope.

But we will be one people, united in glorious harmony as we honor and worship God with one voice. We will perfectly and gloriously bear God's image together as we direct one another's minds, hearts, and affections in wonderous joy toward our Creator and Savior.

Our calling as icons of Christ doesn't go away in the new heavens and new earth. We will not stop being and bearing God's image, because it's an enduring reality of what it means to be human. Take a moment to think about all the ways that sin, temptation, and the effects of God's curse on sin has made life painful and difficult. In glory, we will be righteous as Christ Jesus is righteous. We will not be plagued with sinful temptations. There will be no more conflicts with other people, and suspicion of other nations or cultures will be erased. We will be free from physical pain, and we will enjoy perfect intimacy with our God—Father, Son, and Holy Spirit. This is God's promise and our destiny. As Paul wrote, "I consider that our present sufferings are not worth comparing with the glory that will be revealed in us" (Romans 8:18).

GOD'S JUDGMENT OF SIN AND DEATH

> He said to me: "It is done. I am the Alpha and the Omega, the Beginning and the End. To the thirsty I will give water without cost from the spring of the water of life. Those who are victorious will inherit all this, and I will be their God and they will be my children. But the cowardly, the unbelieving, the vile, the murderers, the sexually immoral, those who practice magic arts, the idolaters and all liars—they will be consigned to the fiery lake of burning sulfur. This is the second death." (Revelation 21:6–8)

Think about all the social injustices that we advocate against today. Most of them are truly evil because of the ways they dishonor men and women who bear God's image. Each person carries God-given dignity and honor, yet so many are trampled upon and suffer at the hands of fellow image-bearers. God's judgment will come to defend men and women who bear his image and to punish those who have taken his image and used it for their own glory. His judgment will also put an end to all the seemingly purposeless suffering that's the result of creation's brokenness. Everything will be made right. Until then, let's not mistake God's patience as apathy.

Sin and death always go together. Whenever you see one in the Bible, the other is either nearby or looming in the shadows. They are intimately connected. "The wages of sin is death" (Romans 6:23) is a principle that's baked into our innate sense of justice. This is why we feel such a strong sense of injustice when people commit great sins without any accountability or punishment. And this is why victims of oppression call on God for judgment, to make their oppressors answer for their sins. The final judgment will bring an end to sin and everything it brings, including death itself and rebellion against God.

The book of Revelation is full of symbolic language that describes the final judgment. Although faithful Christians interpret the specific meaning of these symbols differently, most agree that the dragon represents Satan or those who act on his behalf. These dark and demonic forces bring sin, death, and destruction upon God's people until they receive their judgment upon the return of Jesus Christ.

Revelation foretells of the day when the beast and his followers will be conquered, and the people of God will stand victorious. Jesus will return to cast down the dragon and the beast. Those who worship the beast's image rather than embracing their identity as God's image-bearers will also be judged for the ways they've rebelled against God's reign. This victory over the beast and his followers also brings victory over sin and death. Every tear will be wiped away. Every heartache mended. And there will be no more death, for sin has been utterly defeated.

This is why Revelation 21:1 mentions "and there was no longer any sea" in the new heavens and new earth. It's not because God is anti-sailing or hates the water. It's a symbol of God's complete victory over all the spiritual powers who are against him.

In biblical language, the sea usually represents chaos. It's a place demons call home. For example, this is why Legion, the demon who was cast out of a man in Mark 5:1–13, entered into pigs and ran into the sea. The demons weren't trying to kill the pigs; they were trying to go home. The beast comes out of the sea in Revelation 13:1, and 20:13 describes the sea as containing the souls of the dead.

This is also why it was so astounding to the disciples when Jesus walks on water (Matthew 14:22–33) and calms the storm by simply telling it to be still (Matthew 8:23–27). The disciples began to worship him, because it was representative of his authority over all creation, including the sea. There is no potential for future rebellion or corruption in the new heavens and new earth. There is no longer a sea because God has completely defeated his enemies. He doesn't simply stand on it in victory. It has been lit on fire and turned to glass, and those who have been faithful to Christ Jesus will stand beside the sea of glass in victory (Revelation 15:2). Secure. In the presence of God with perfect intimacy.

THE PRESENCE OF GOD!

> And I heard a loud voice from the throne saying, "Look! God's dwelling place is now among the people, and he will dwell with them. They will be his people, and God himself will be with them and be their God." (Revelation 21:3)

Ever since Adam and Eve were sent out of the garden of Eden, one of the most repeated promises of God toward the people of Israel is a variation of this: "I will walk among you and be your God, and you will be my people" (Leviticus 26:12; see also Jeremiah 32:38; Ezekiel 37:27; 2 Corinthians 6:16). This was a foundational promise for Israel, and they lived with hopeful expectation that God would be with them. There is no greater comfort or assurance than to be welcomed into the presence of God. This is also why God manifested his presence with Israel during their wilderness wanderings through the cloud by day and pillar of fire at night (Exodus 13:21–22) and why Jesus told his disciples shortly before ascending back to heaven, "I am with you always, to the very end of the age" (Matthew 28:20).

God is present with us in two ways: through his transcendence and immanence. God is present in his transcendence, which describes his presence and authority over all things. This is anchored in God's omnipresence and sovereignty. We read about God's transcendence in verses like Proverbs 15:3 ("The eyes of the LORD are everywhere") and Psalm 139:7–8 ("Where can I flee from your presence? If I go up to the heavens, you are there; if I make my bed in the depths, you are there").

God's immanence has to do with his immediate presence. After Eden, God would appear to people in a vision (Genesis 15:1), send a message to them through an angel (Daniel 9:20–23), appear to them through "the angel of the LORD" (1 Kings 19:7), or even appear through other physical manifestations (Exodus 3). But God's people did not live in the full and intimate presence of God like Adam and Eve. Neither did they have the Holy Spirit living in them, like Christians do today (1 Corinthians 6:19). They hungered and yearned for the presence of God and for everything it meant. Paul lifts our eyes to our future hope by telling us, "For now we see only a reflection as in a mirror; then we shall see face to face. Now I know in part; then I shall know fully, even as I am fully known" (1 Corinthians 13:12).

Revelation 21–22 are among the most beautiful chapters in the Bible because here this longing for the immanent presence of God is finally fulfilled. God will be fully and eternally with people, and it will not be taken away or diminished. As pastor Tim Keller has written, "Heaven will make amends for everything."[3]

Every heartache, every tear, and every moment of loneliness, anxiety, and doubt will be satisfied and wiped away by the nail-pierced hands of Jesus Christ. We will live so securely and joyfully in the presence of God that everything we've endured in this life will be worth it.

Truly, "our present sufferings are not worth comparing with the glory that will be revealed in us" (Romans 8:18).

Everything God has promised will be fulfilled in the glory of the new heavens and new earth. We will eat, sing, play, and worship together with one voice, celebrating our great God. And we will bear God's image in such a way that leads all creation to shout in praise, "Hallelujah! For our Lord God Almighty reigns" (Revelation 19:6). We will bear God's image perfectly to one another and to all creation as holy displays of God's glory and goodness.

Gospel Clarity: The Glorified Image

Christian hope is so much more than rescue from the judgment our sin deserves. Our hope is to be with God, face-to-face, with perfect and complete intimacy. Our hope is to become perfectly iconic: to be and bear God's image with glory and goodness that prompts us and all creation to burst forth with love and joy because of who God is.

Your life carries God-given dignity and honor because you bear God's image. I'm praying this glimpse of the glory to come will give you strength and endurance to keep your eyes on Jesus Christ when life is difficult. There are moments when every Christian wonders, *Is this worth it?* I hope this chapter helps you answer that question with a resounding "Yes!"

QUESTIONS FOR REFLECTION

1. When you think about heaven and eternity, what typically comes to mind? How is that similar or different from what this chapter describes?

2. How can this vision inspire you to faithfully walk with Christ, even when life is difficult, confusing, or painful?

3. What are you most looking forward to about living in glory, in the perfect presence of God?

Conclusion
Iconic for Life

It's not difficult to look at the world around you and to wonder, *I don't think it's supposed to be like this. What went wrong?* You were created for intimacy: To know God and be known by him. To walk in deep fellowship with God, with other people, and with creation. To be and bear God's glory and goodness in this world.

We have forgotten more than who we are. We've forgotten what we are and what it means to be a human being. This is why there is so much unraveling all around us. Conversations about sexuality, gender, race, abortion, disabilities, mental health, and environmentalism have become marked by confusion and conflict. When there's no shared foundation, all that remains is my opinion versus yours. But when we remember our Creator and what he created humanity to be, these issues begin to come into focus.

God created us male and female, in his image. We are living icons who represent his glory and goodness in this world, in order that all creation would praise our holy God. As his image-bearers and icons, we share some of his attributes, which he has embedded within our humanity. This is why every human being is iconic, to some degree. Grandparents who are living with dementia, inmates who have committed heinous crimes, and atheists who openly mock God's existence still bear God's image because it's foundational to our humanity.

The gospel of Jesus Christ makes us iconic according to God's design. This is the work of God in us that renews our love for God and conforms us day by day into the image of Christ. If we want to see what it looks like to perfectly bear God's image, then we need to look to Jesus. In all the ways the first Adam failed, Jesus Christ, the "second Adam," succeeded, and we share in that victory through the gift of the Holy Spirit. Jesus has conquered sin and death through the cross and will return again to glorify his beloved creation, including us! We will be perfectly human and holy. There will be no more loneliness, sickness, suffering, injustice, or death. We will bear God's image together, with perfect harmony, in the very presence of God.

This is our story. This is *your* story. This is what God created humanity to enjoy. You fit in here somewhere. So as you're navigating your questions about life, meaning, purpose, and belonging, ask the big questions of life with confidence in what you are: an icon of Christ.

I hope this book has helped you see the gospel is an invitation, not a theory. It's an invitation to meet Jesus and rediscover what you are as an image-bearer of God's glory and goodness. It's also an invitation to be restored into the image of Christ so that everything in your life—relationships, work, studies, recreation, etc.—can be used to carry out God's intended mission for you: prompting others toward worship because they see the glory and goodness of God in you.

QUESTIONS FOR REFLECTION:

1. What does it mean for people to be created in the image of God, and how does that help you understand what it means to follow Jesus?
2. Name two or three ways this book has strengthened your understanding of what it means to be human and to become more like Jesus.
3. What's one big lesson from this book that you hope to remember and apply?

Acknowledgments

My name is on the cover, but this book is the result of many contributions. First and foremost is my wife, Tracy, and my kids, Matthew and Hannah. You've sacrificed family time so I could write this book. And you've pulled me away from the computer when needed to keep me grounded. Your love is a glowing icon of Christ's love to me. I am so blessed.

Thanks to series editor Samuel Bierig for inviting me to contribute. I'm continually thankful for Barbara Juliani and Ruth Castle for their encouragement and for their leadership at New Growth Press, a rare publisher who believes in publishing theologically rich books for youth and young adults. Brandon Peterson and Josh Cooley offered keen edits that helped shape what I wrote into a form that is accessible and clear. And finally, thanks to Dan Stelzer and Derek Thornton for patiently working with me to design the right cover for this book.

Endnotes

Introduction

1. For more on this emphasis, see Carmen Joy Imes, *Being God's Image: Why Creation Still Matters* (InterVarsity, 2023).

2. A different Hebrew word is used in this passage for *image* because it's a specific word for an idol (an image that you worship).

Chapter 2

1. Lisa Littman, "Correction: Parent reports of adolescents and young adults perceived to show signs of a rapid onset of gender dysphoria," *PLOS One* 14, no. 3, March 19, 2019, https://doi.org/10.1371/journal.pone.0214157.

Chapter 6

1. Sally Lloyd-Jones, *The Jesus Storybook Bible: Every Story Whispers His Name* (Zonderkidz, 2007).

Chapter 7

1. If you became a Christian during one of these types of messages, then I think that's wonderful! Please don't let this clarification about the gospel make you doubt your salvation. God often uses incomplete gospel presentations to do a miraculous work in peoples' lives because he's just that eager to save us! My intent is gospel clarity, not theological nitpickiness. So if your faith has grown and matured after this type of message, then praise the Lord and know that I'm cheering you on.

Chapter 8

1. I'm not implying that Paul intentionally aligned each fruit of the Spirit with a communicable attribute of God. He might have, but I doubt it. I'm simply highlighting that the Holy Spirit led Paul to describe Christian sanctification in a way that conforms them into the image of God, which is anchored in what theologians have labeled the communicable attributes of God.

Chapter 9

1. There is some debate on this topic because there isn't a Bible verse that directly addresses this issue. But the majority of Christians have taken the position that disabilities are healed in the new heavens and new earth.

2. Thomas's unbelief that Jesus rose from the grave and his recognition of Jesus's body through the proof of his nail-pierced hands go hand in hand. If Jesus looked exactly the same, then Thomas might not have insisted on seeing Jesus's hands.

3. Timothy Keller, *Walking with God Through Pain and Suffering* (Penguin, 2013), 13.